Here Be Dragons

Coloring Book — Two

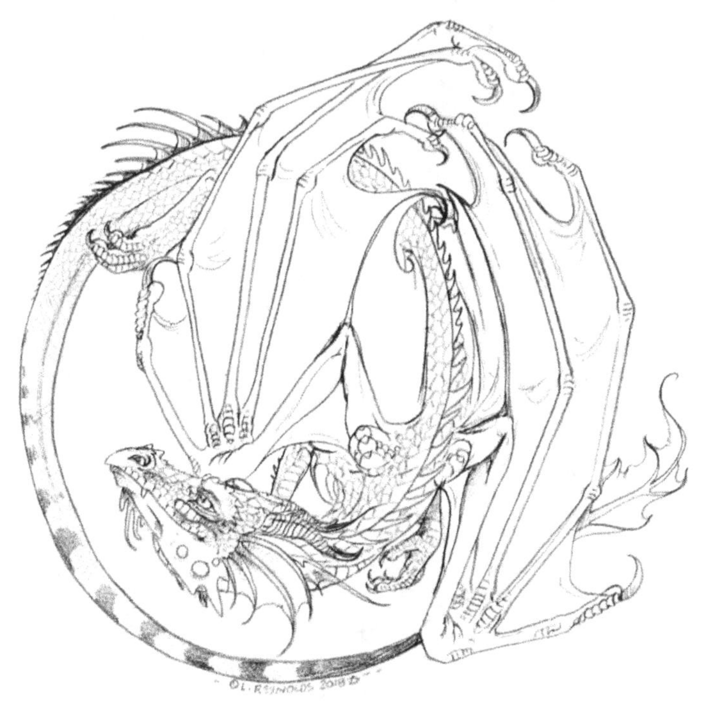

The Fantasy Art of Laura Reynolds

Design Editing by Baer Charlton

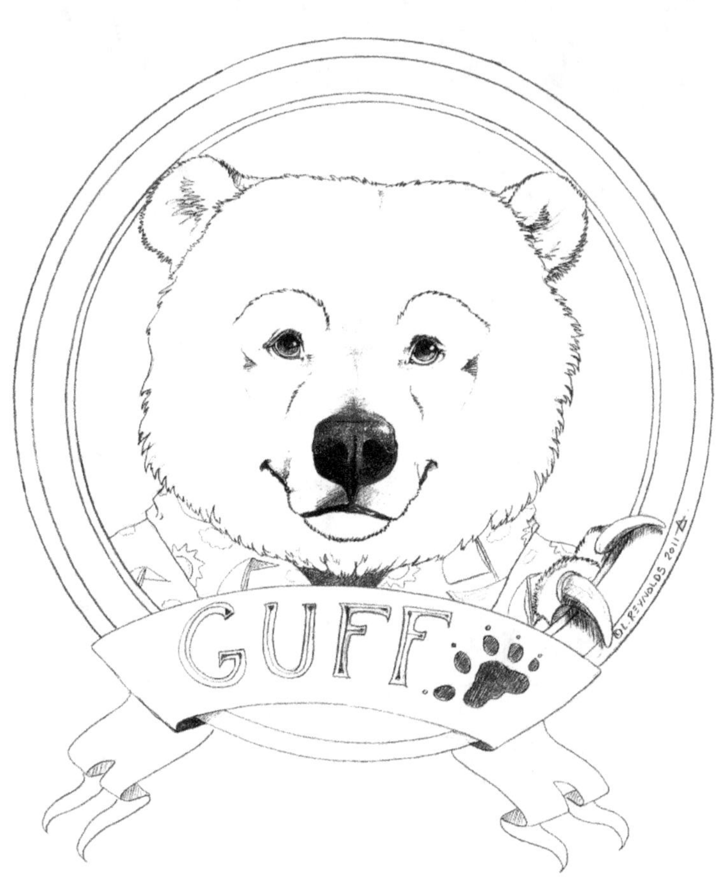
GUFF

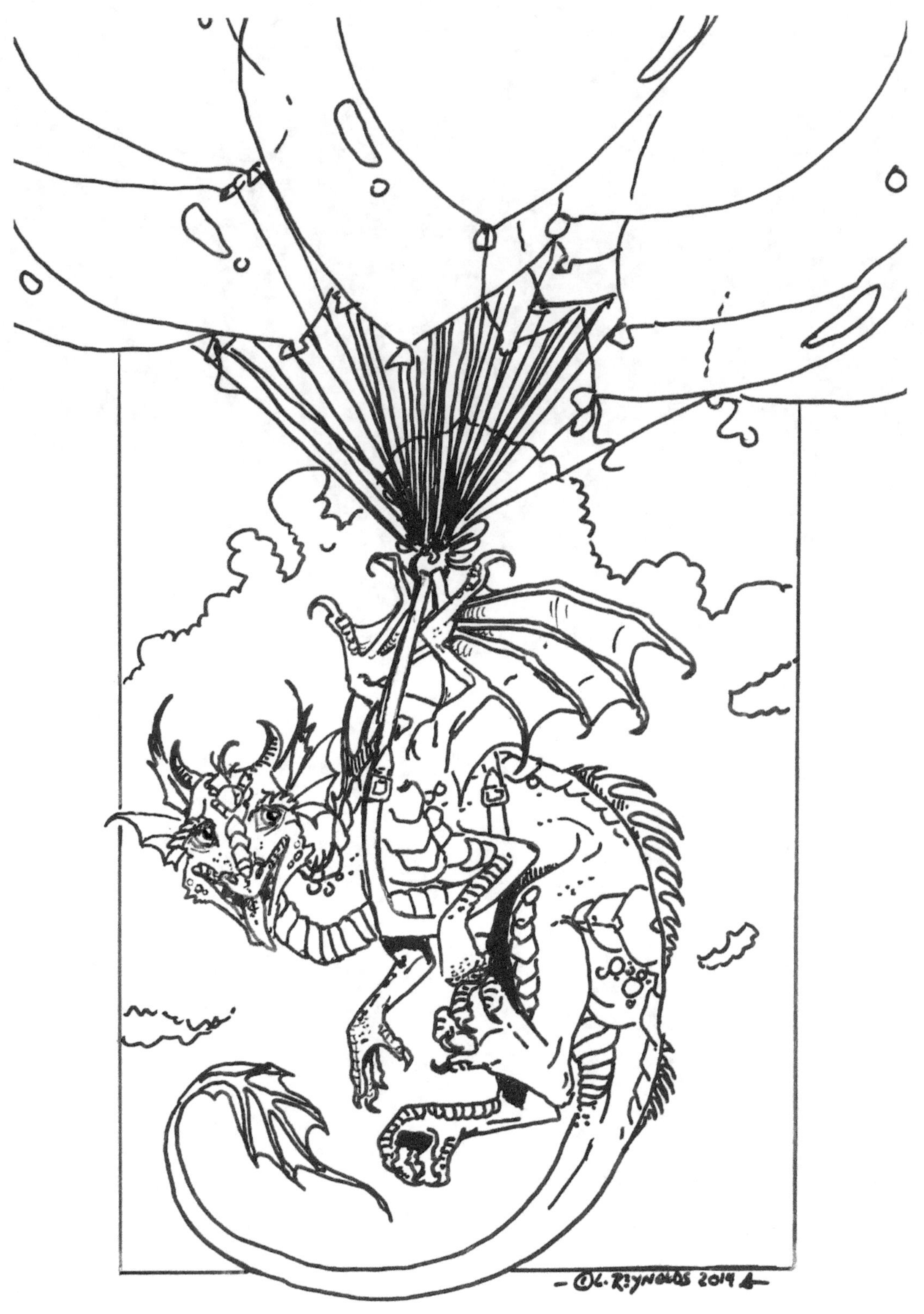

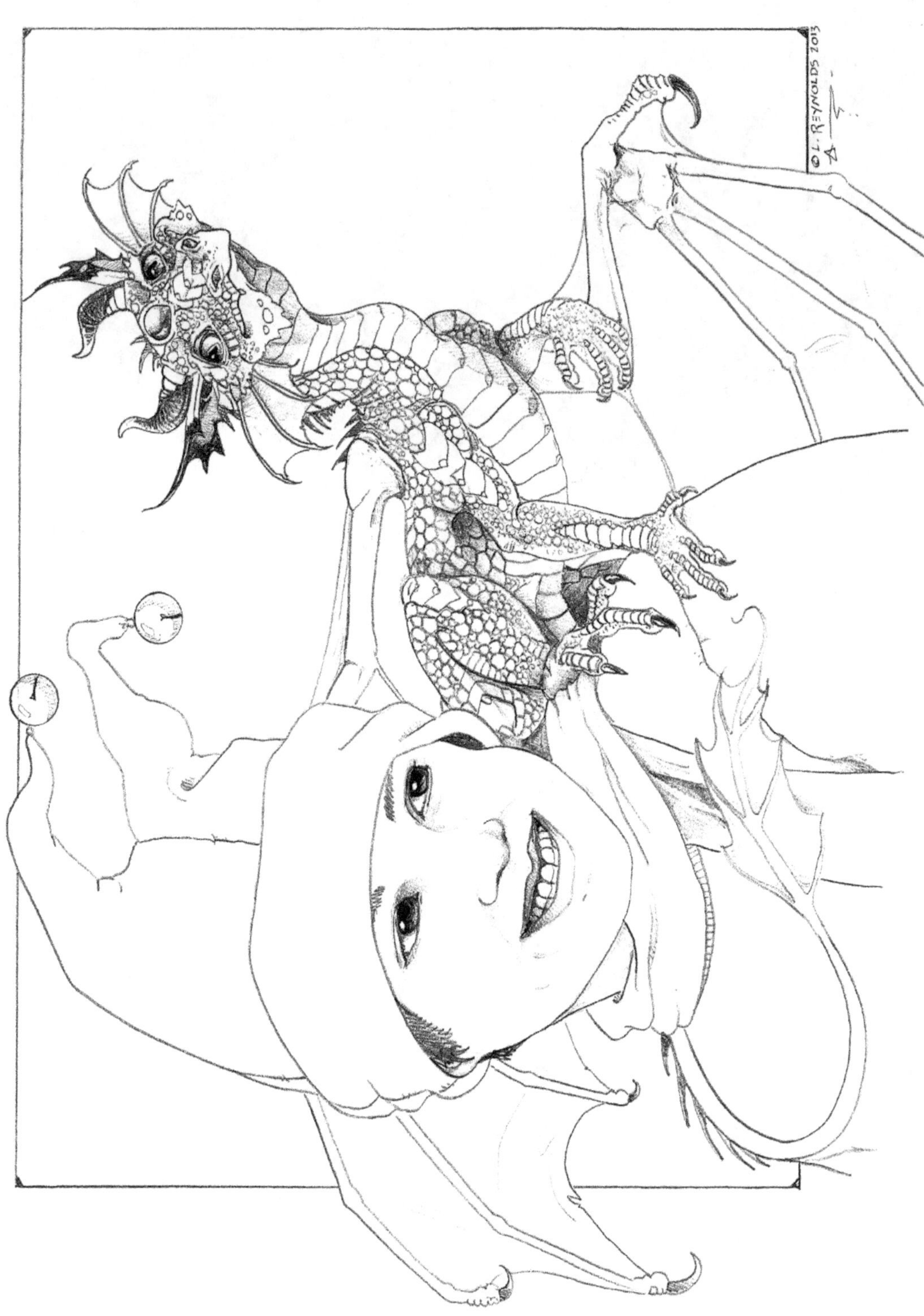

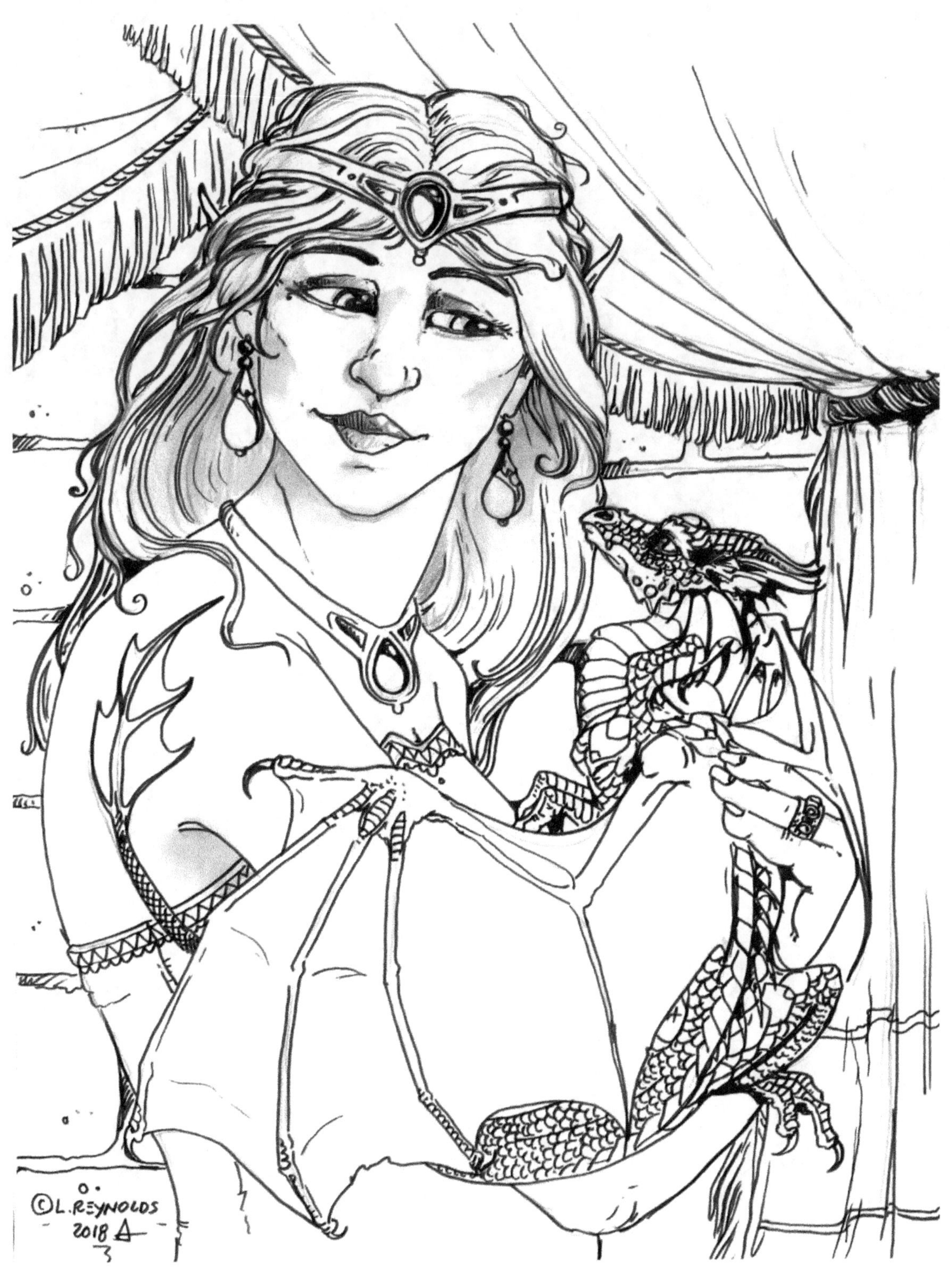
©L.Reynolds
2018

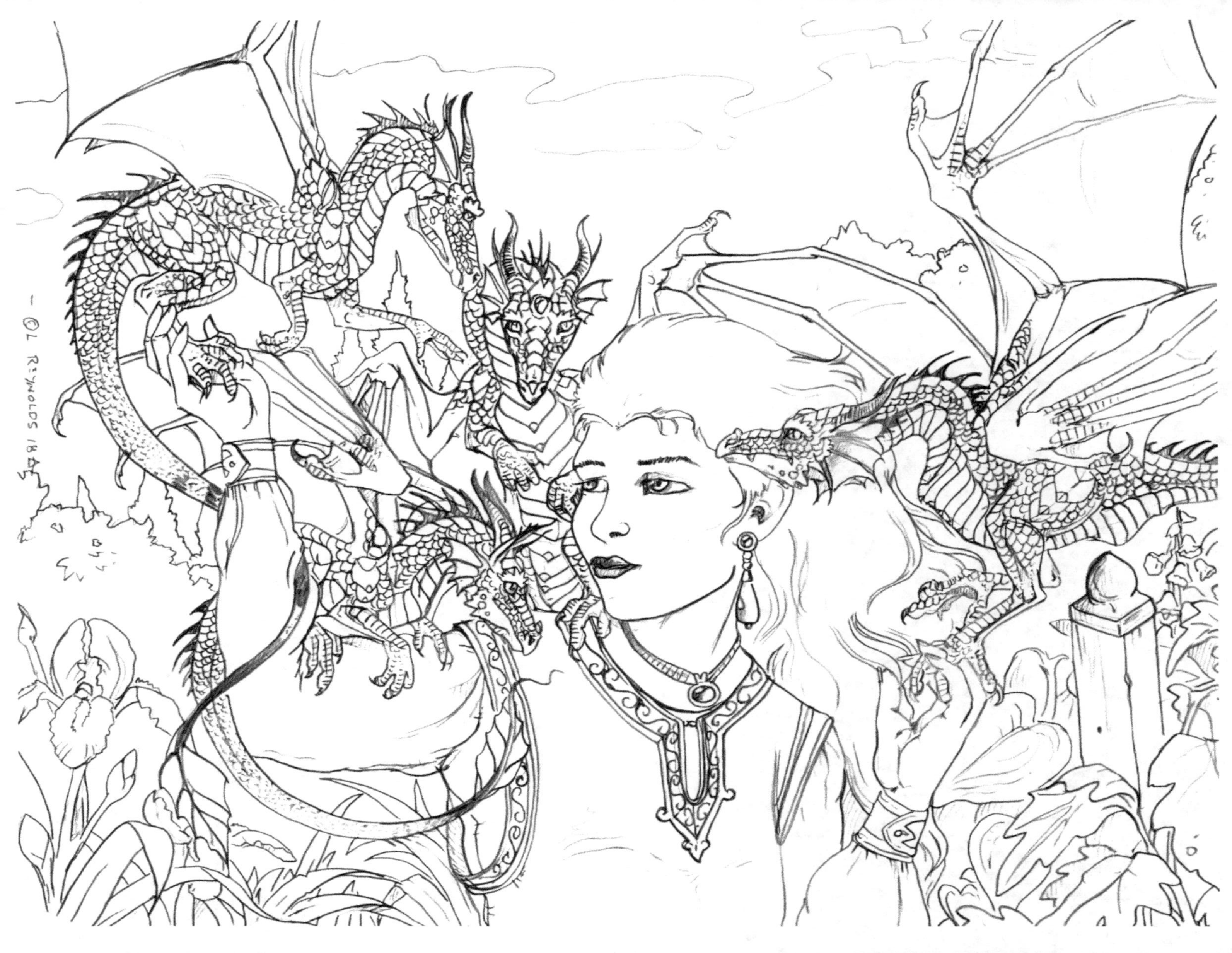
© L REYNOLDS 18

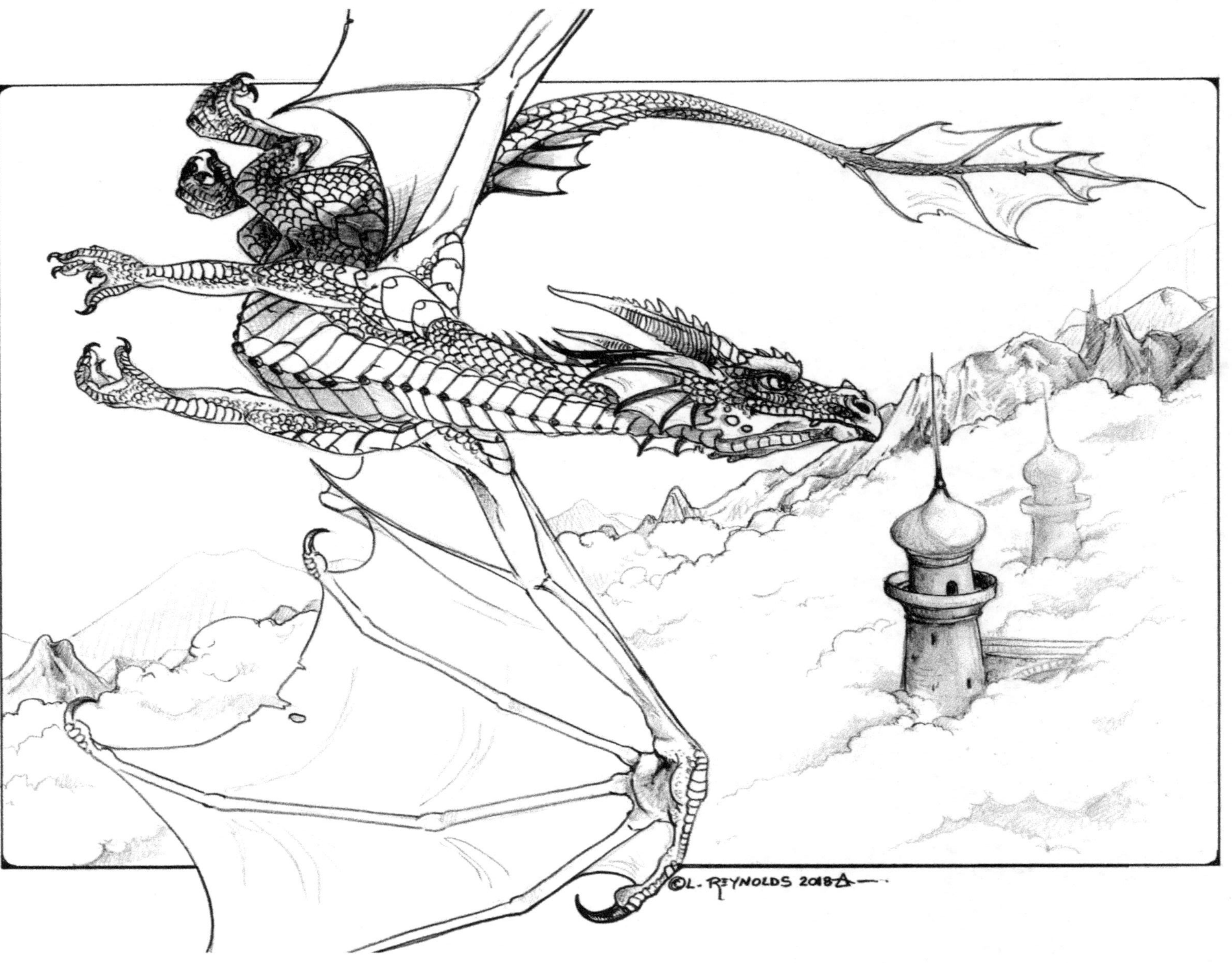
©L. REYNOLDS 2018

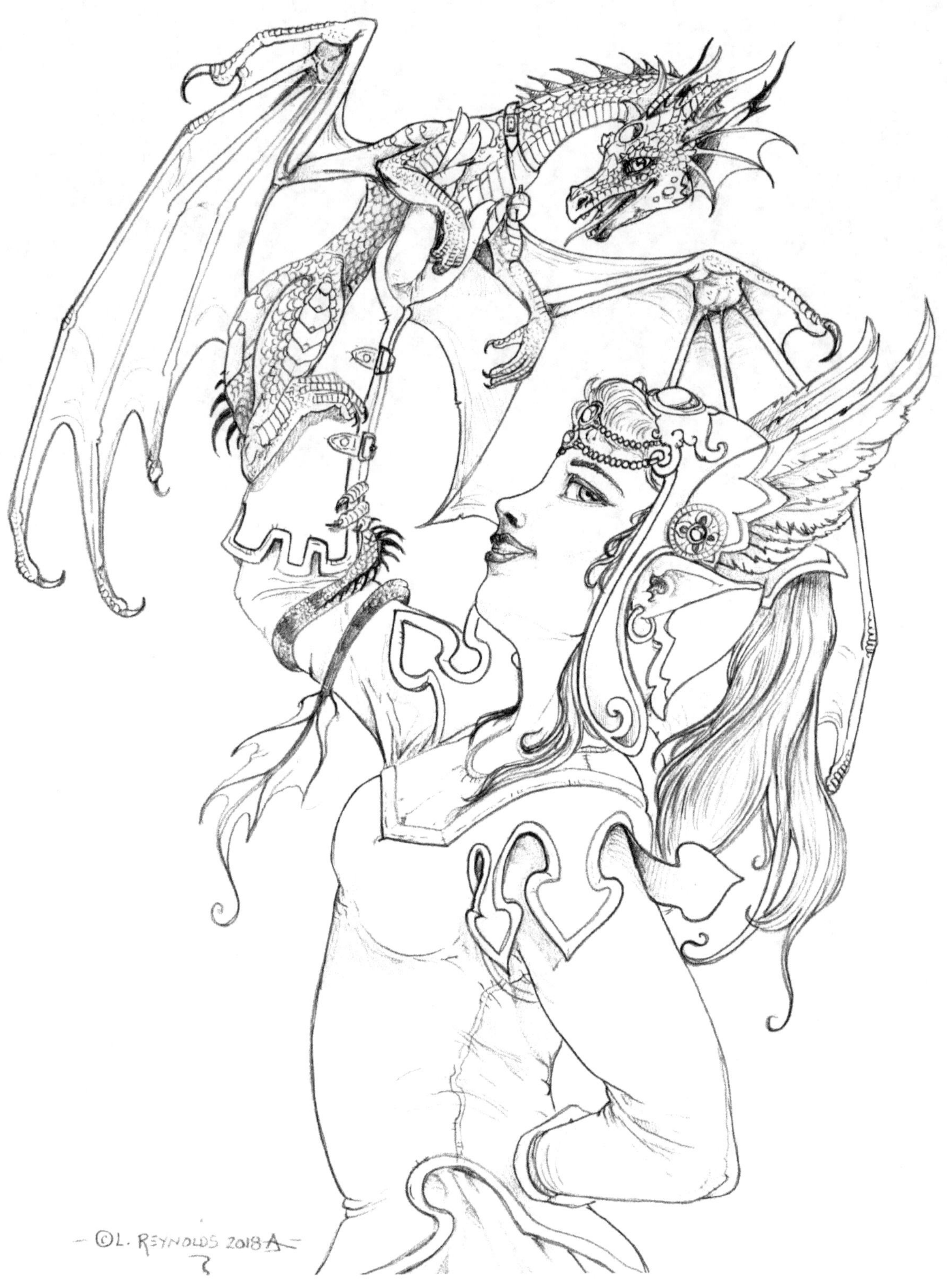

©L. REYNOLDS 2018 A

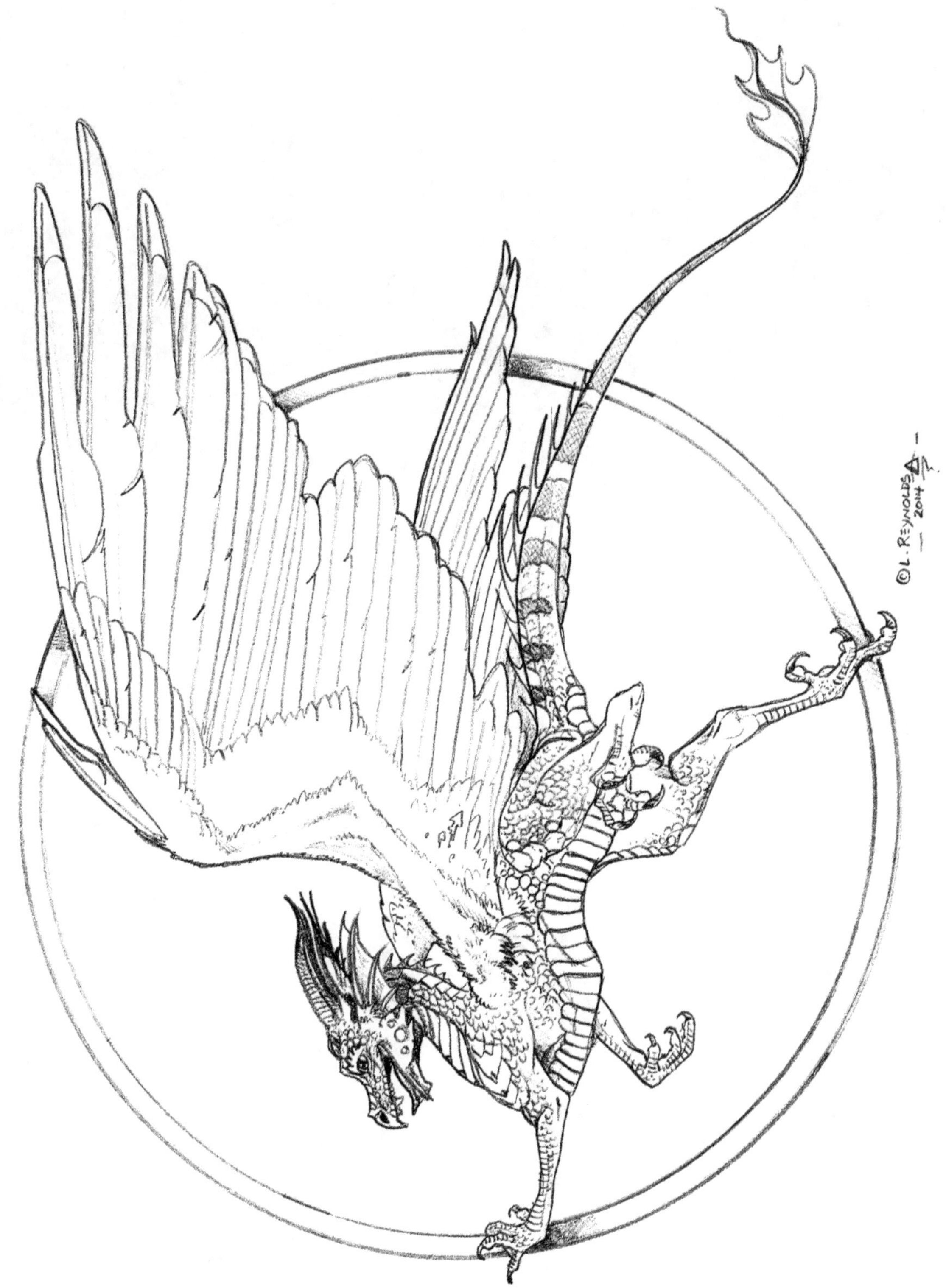

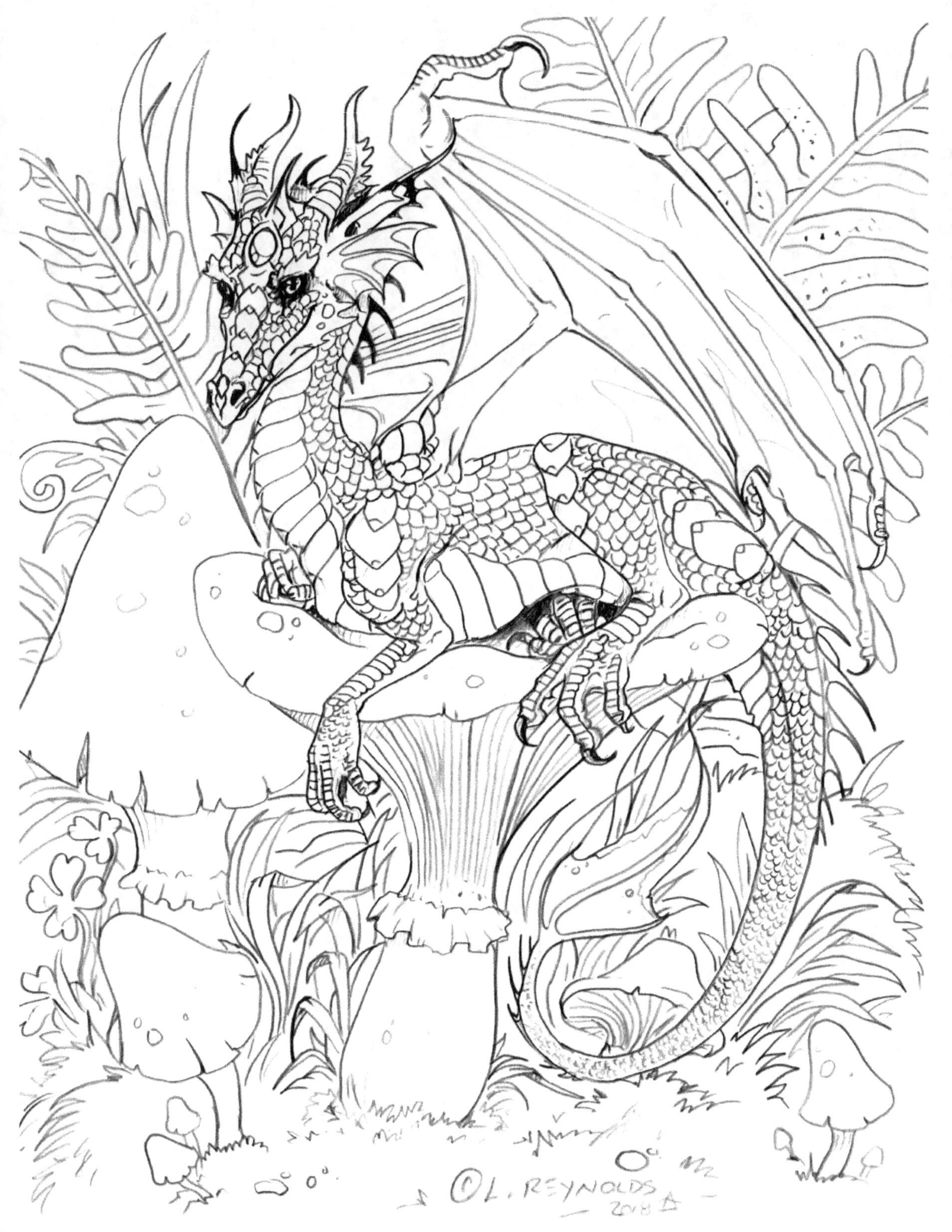
©L. REYNOLDS
2018

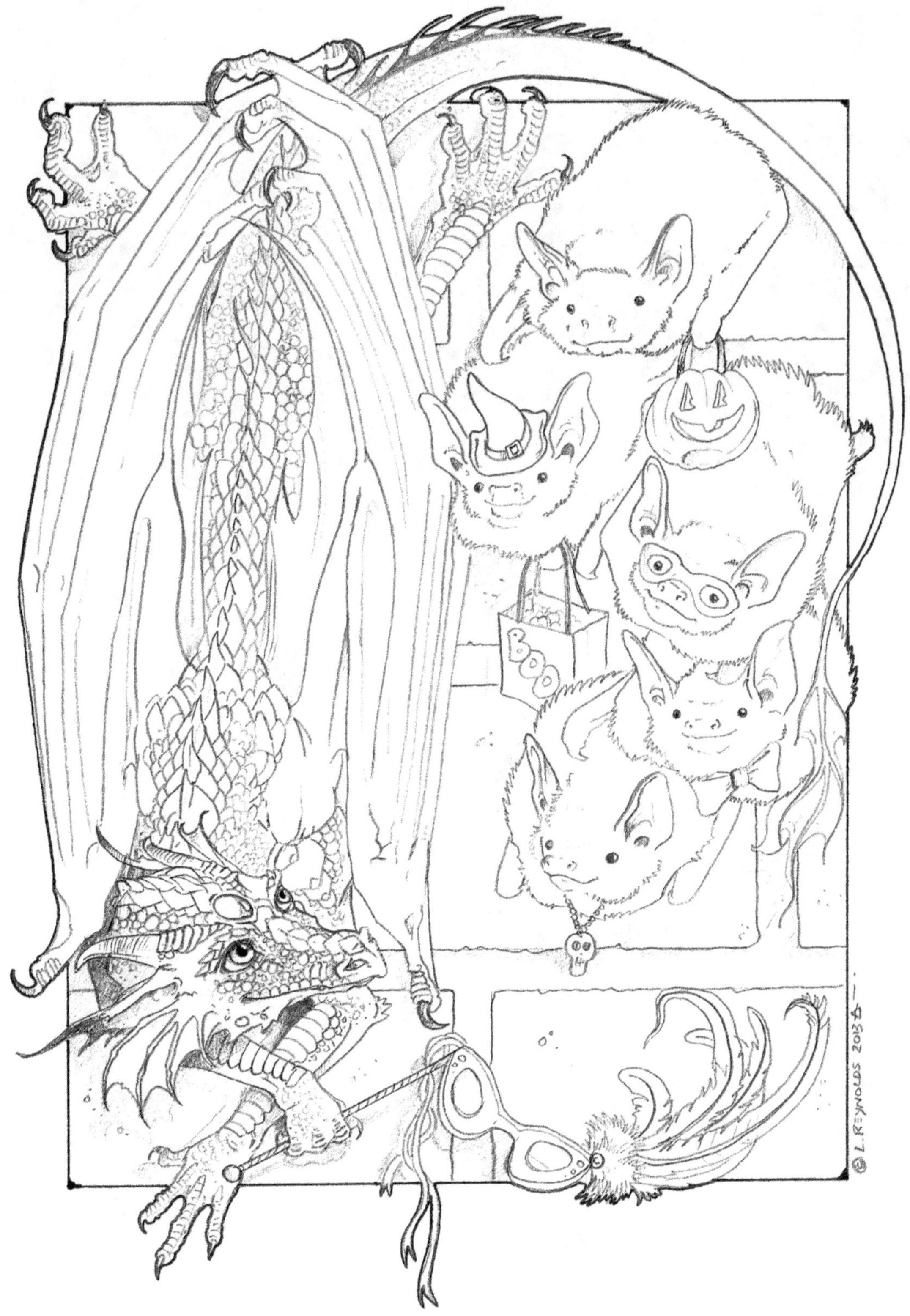

BOO
© L. REYNOLDS 2013

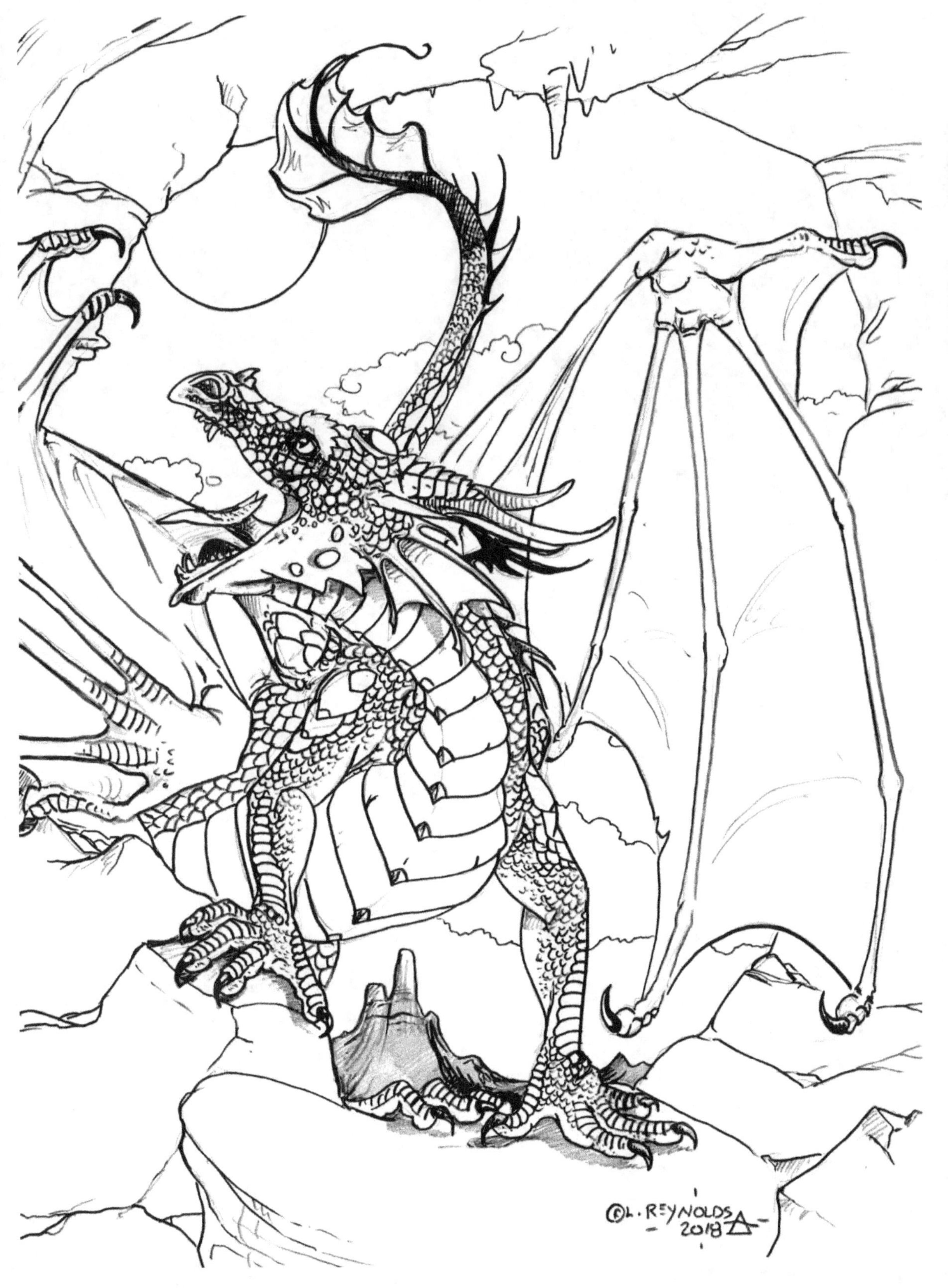
©L. REYNOLDS
2018

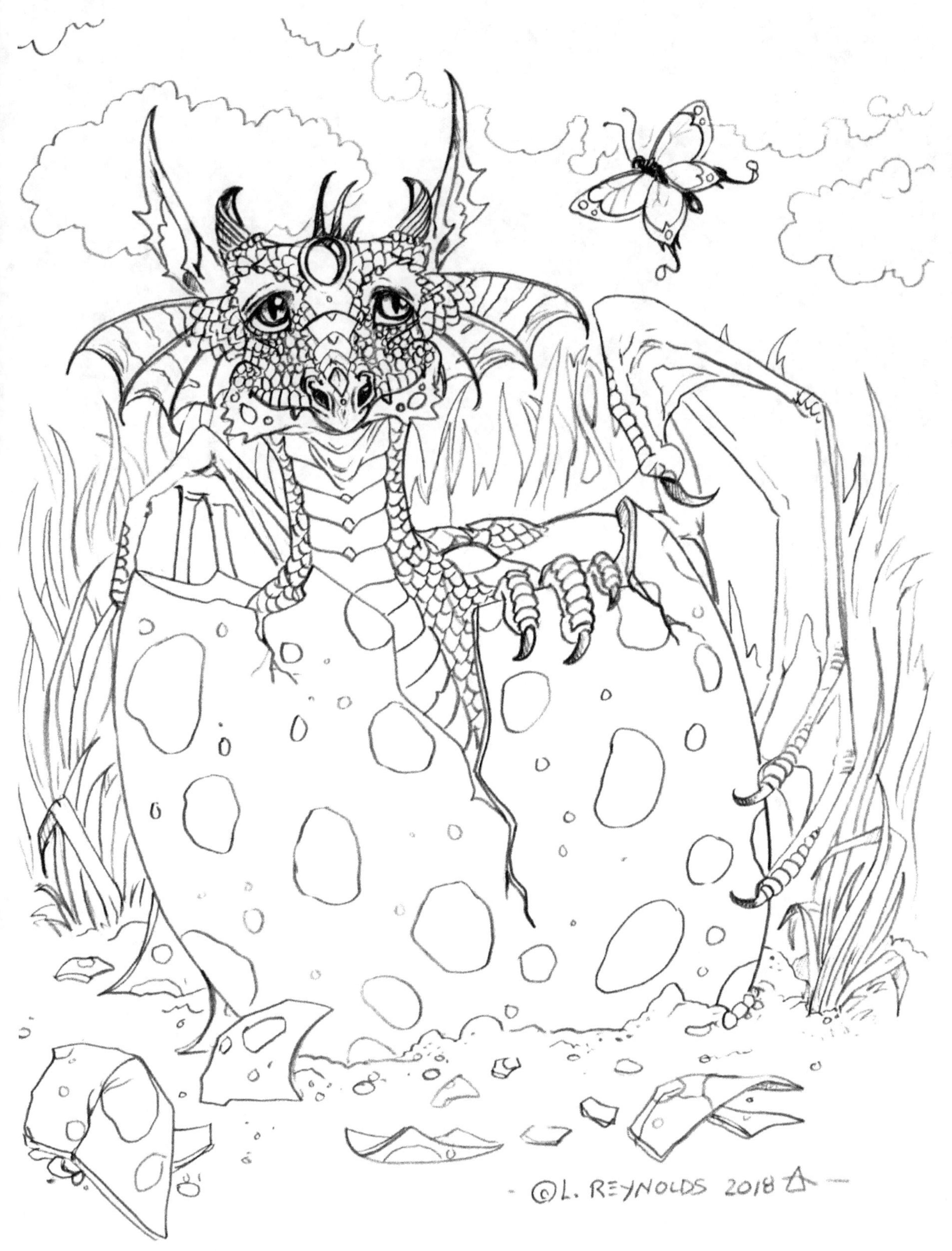
©L. REYNOLDS 2018

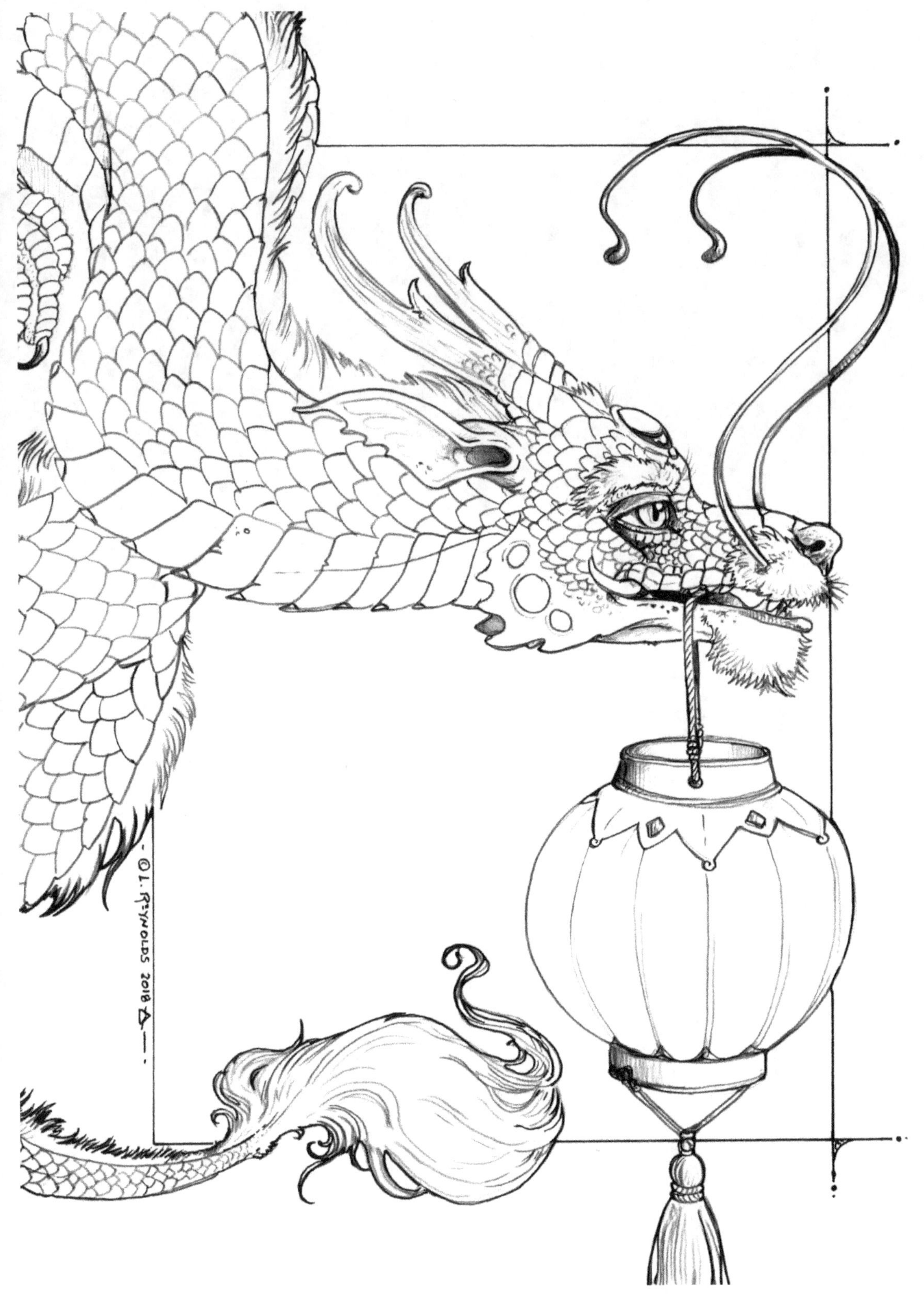

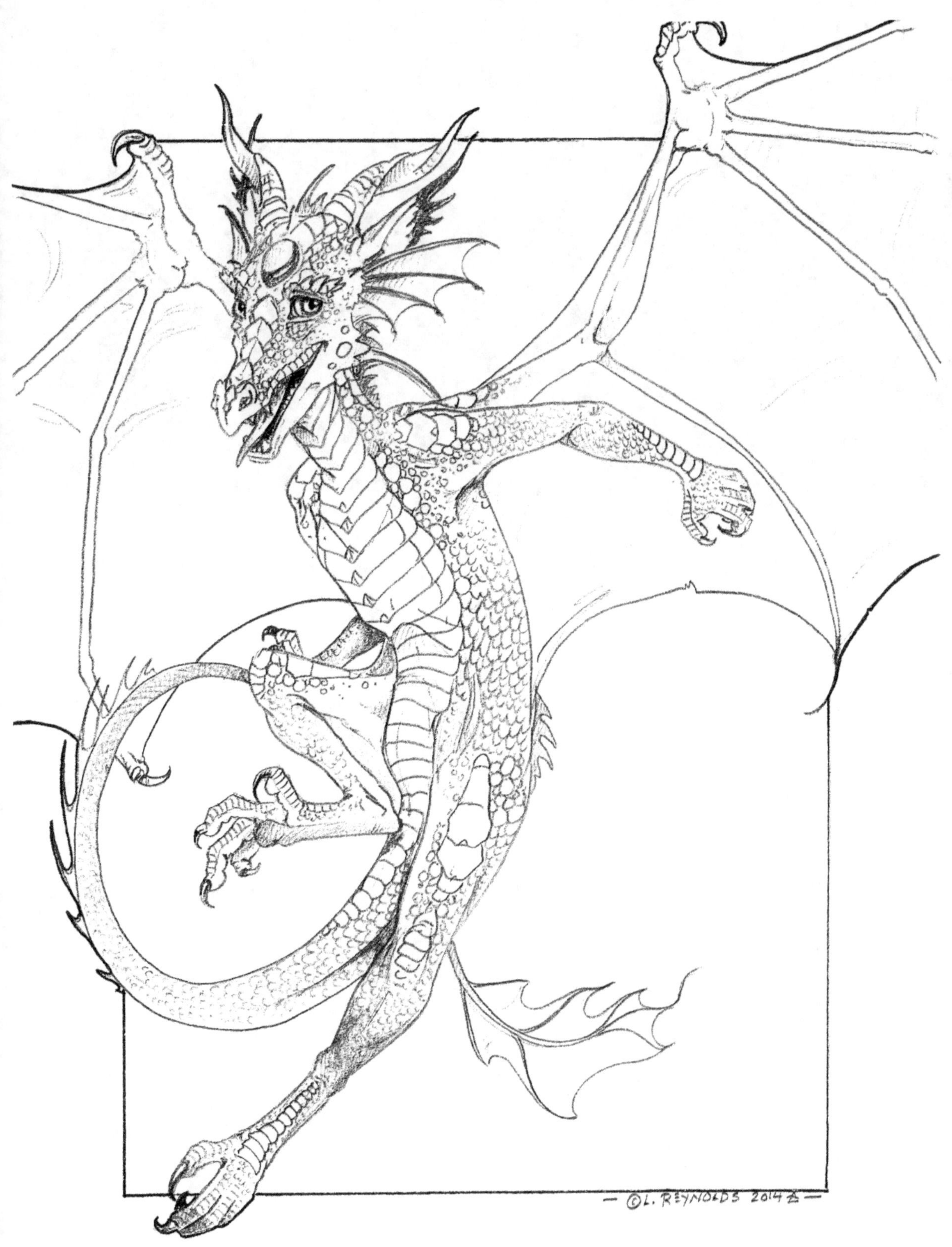

©L. REYNOLDS 2014

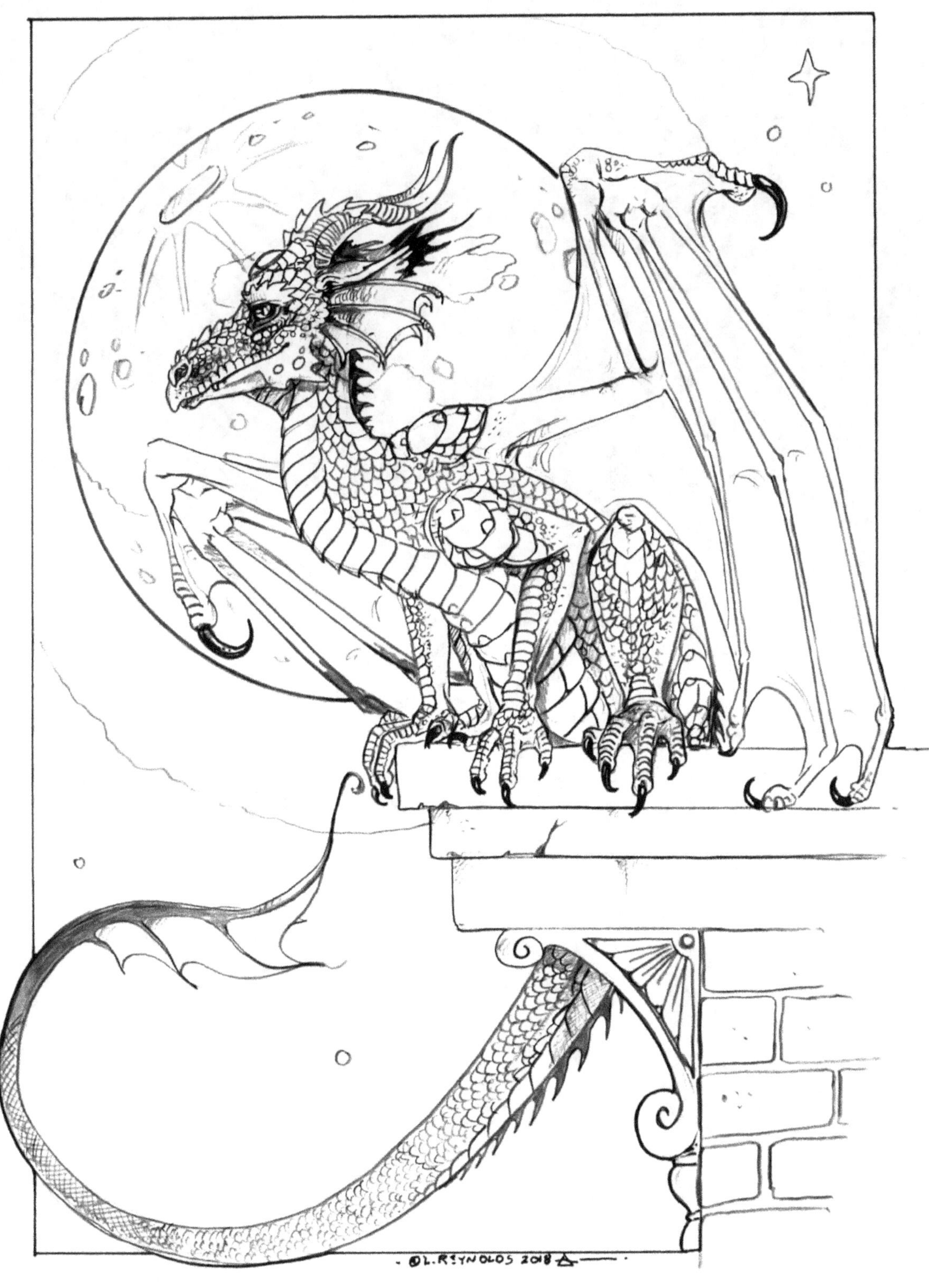
©L.REYNOLDS 2018

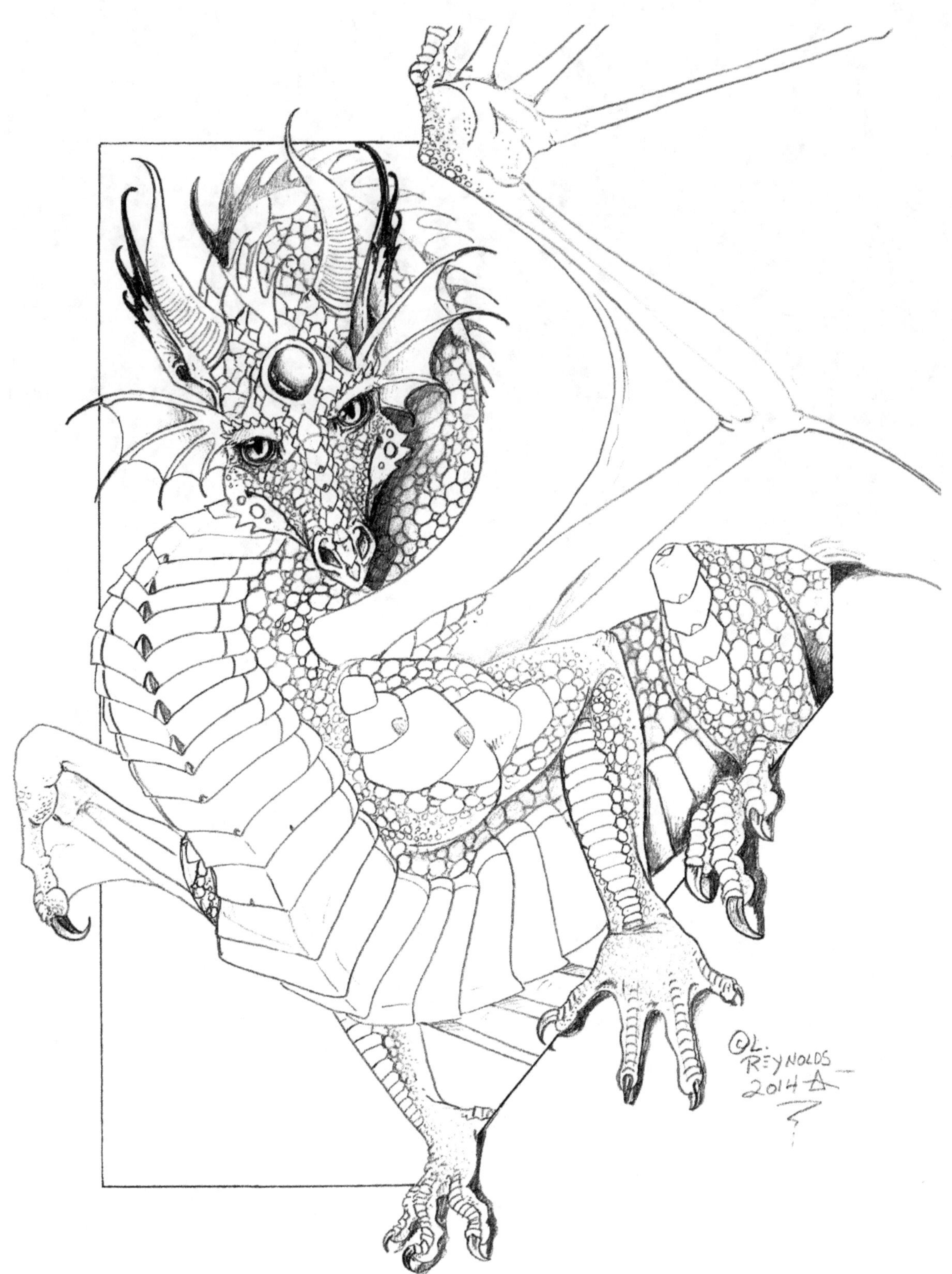
©L. Reynolds
2014

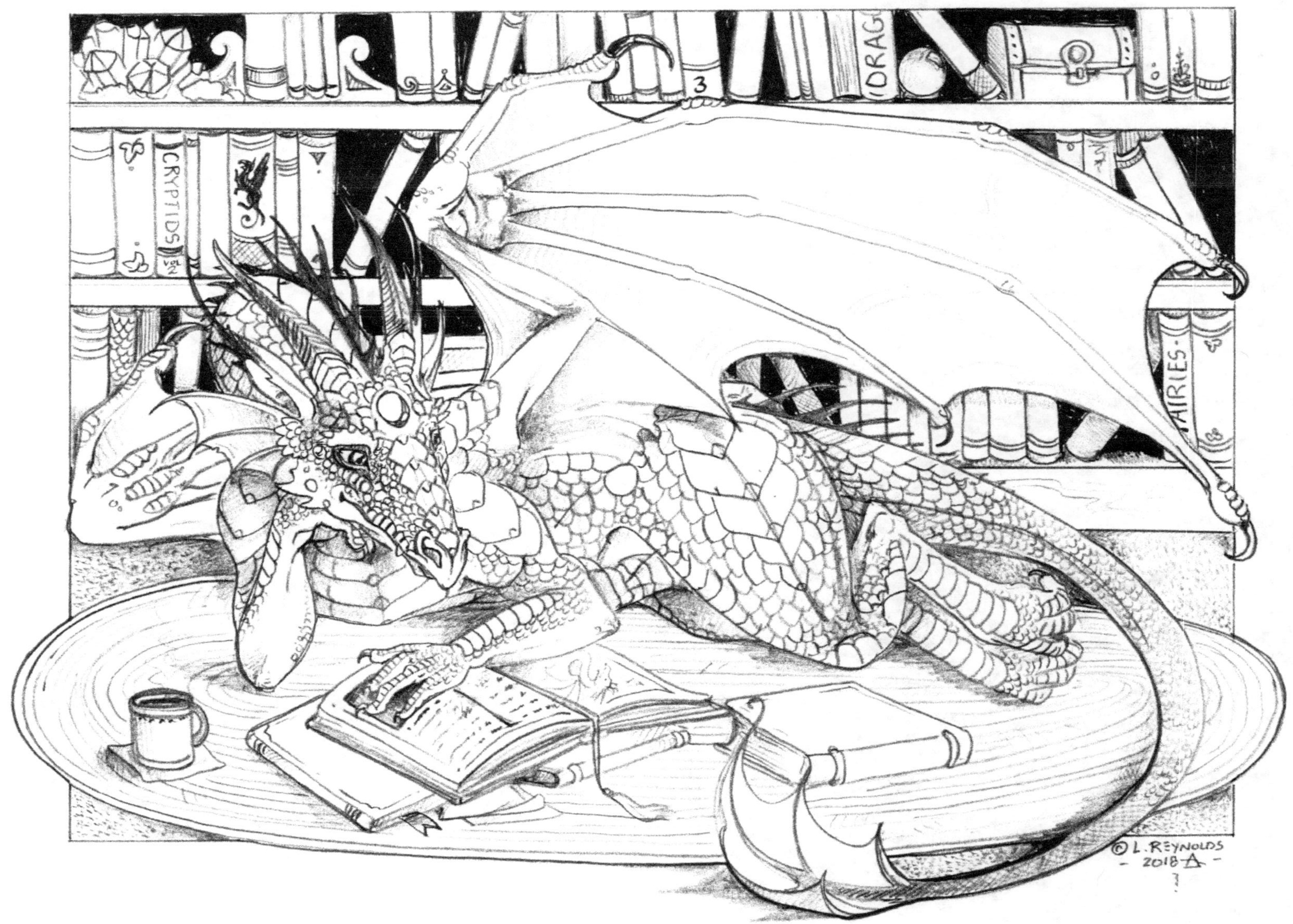
DRAG
CRYPTIDS
·FAIRIES·
© L. REYNOLDS
- 2018 -

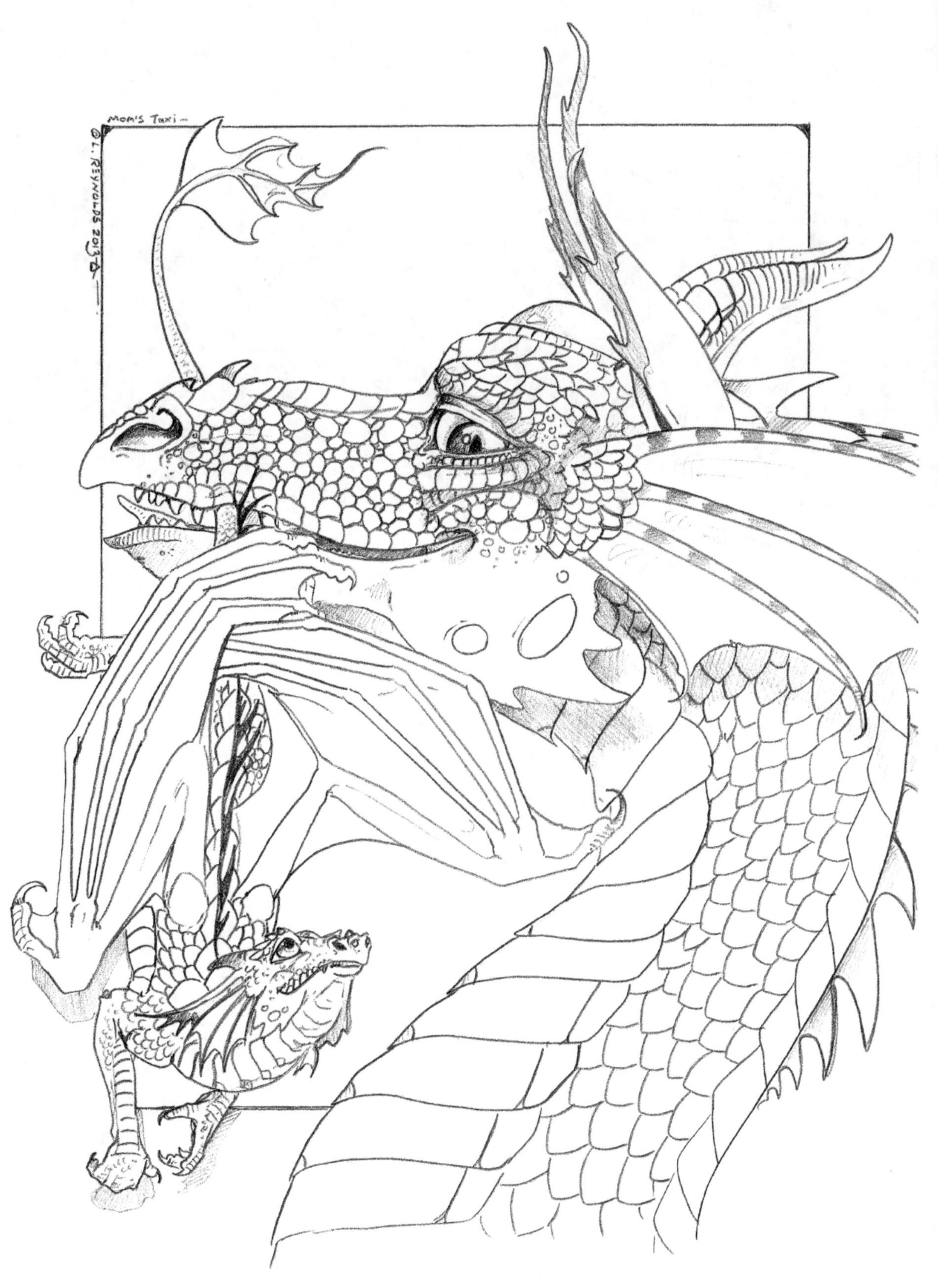
Mom's Taxi
© L. Reynolds 2013

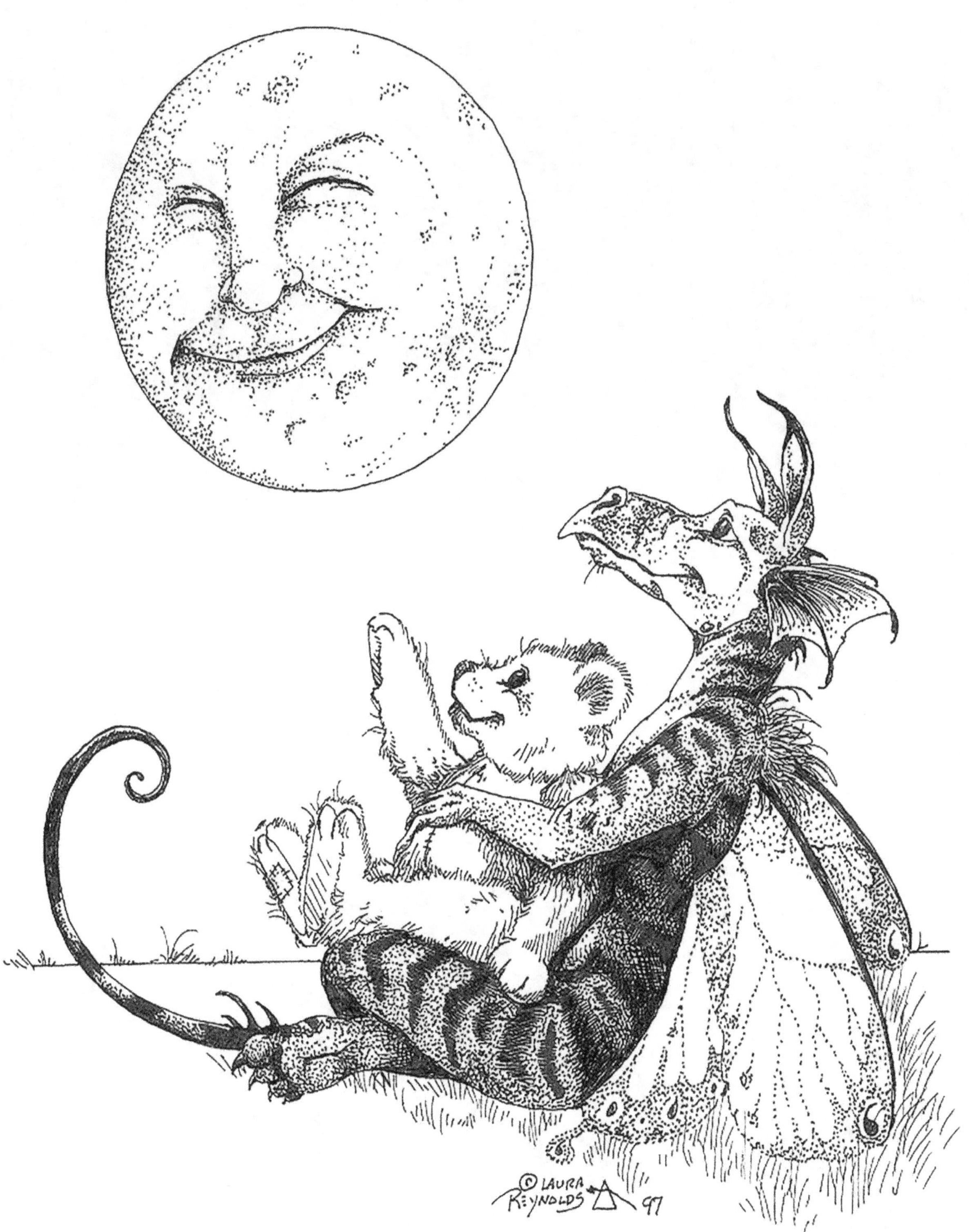

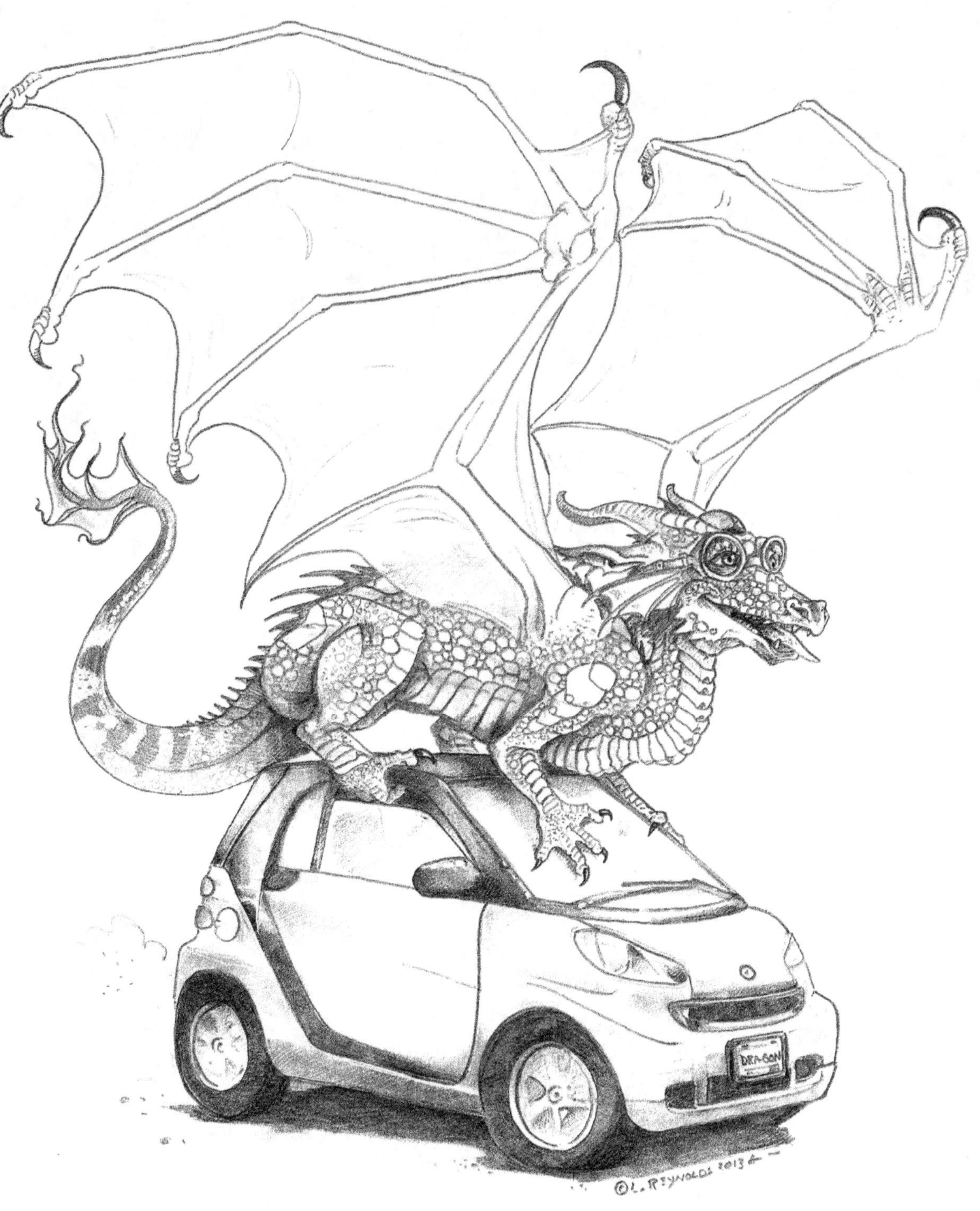

DRA-GON
© L. REYNOLDS 2013

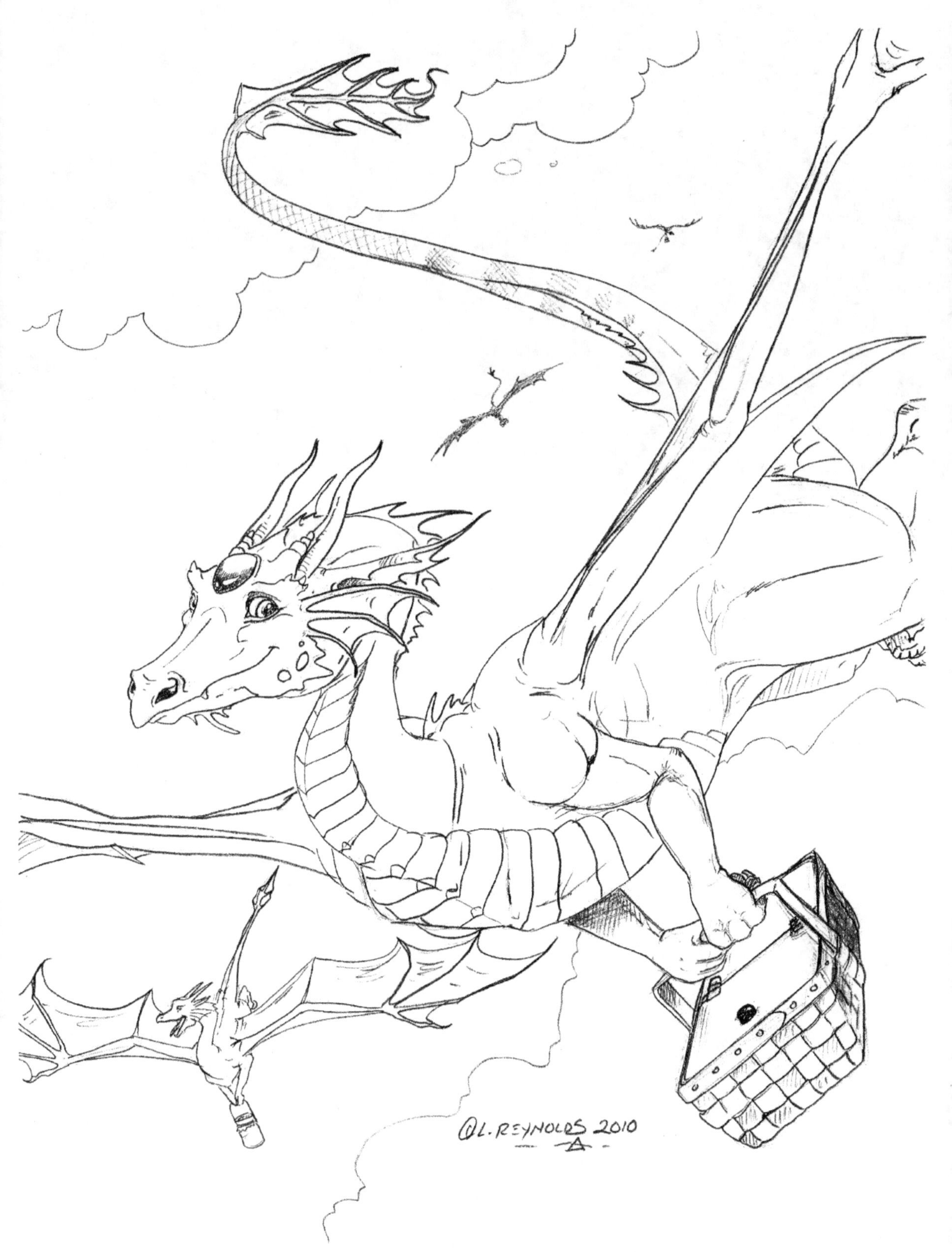
©L. REYNOLDS 2010

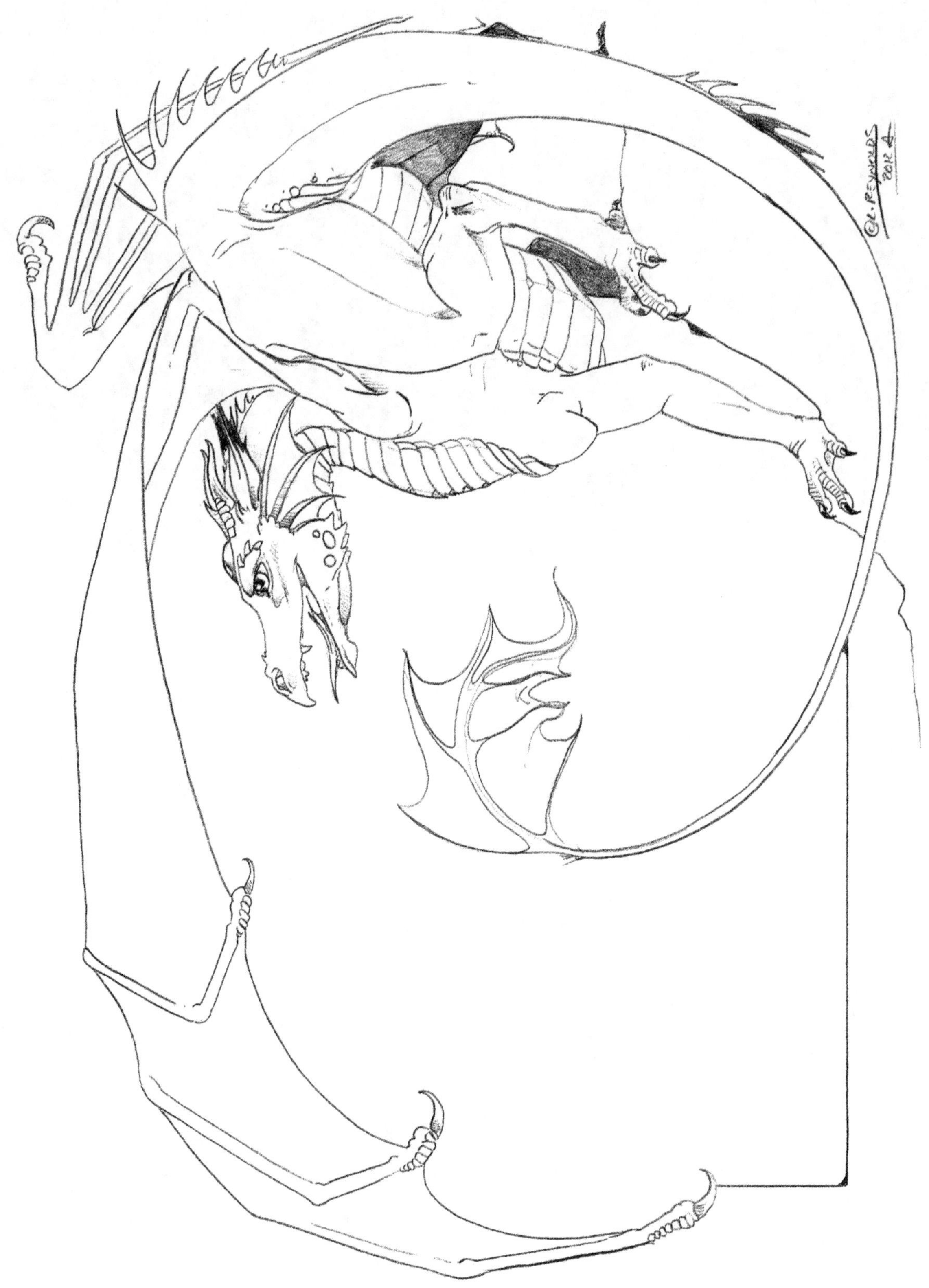

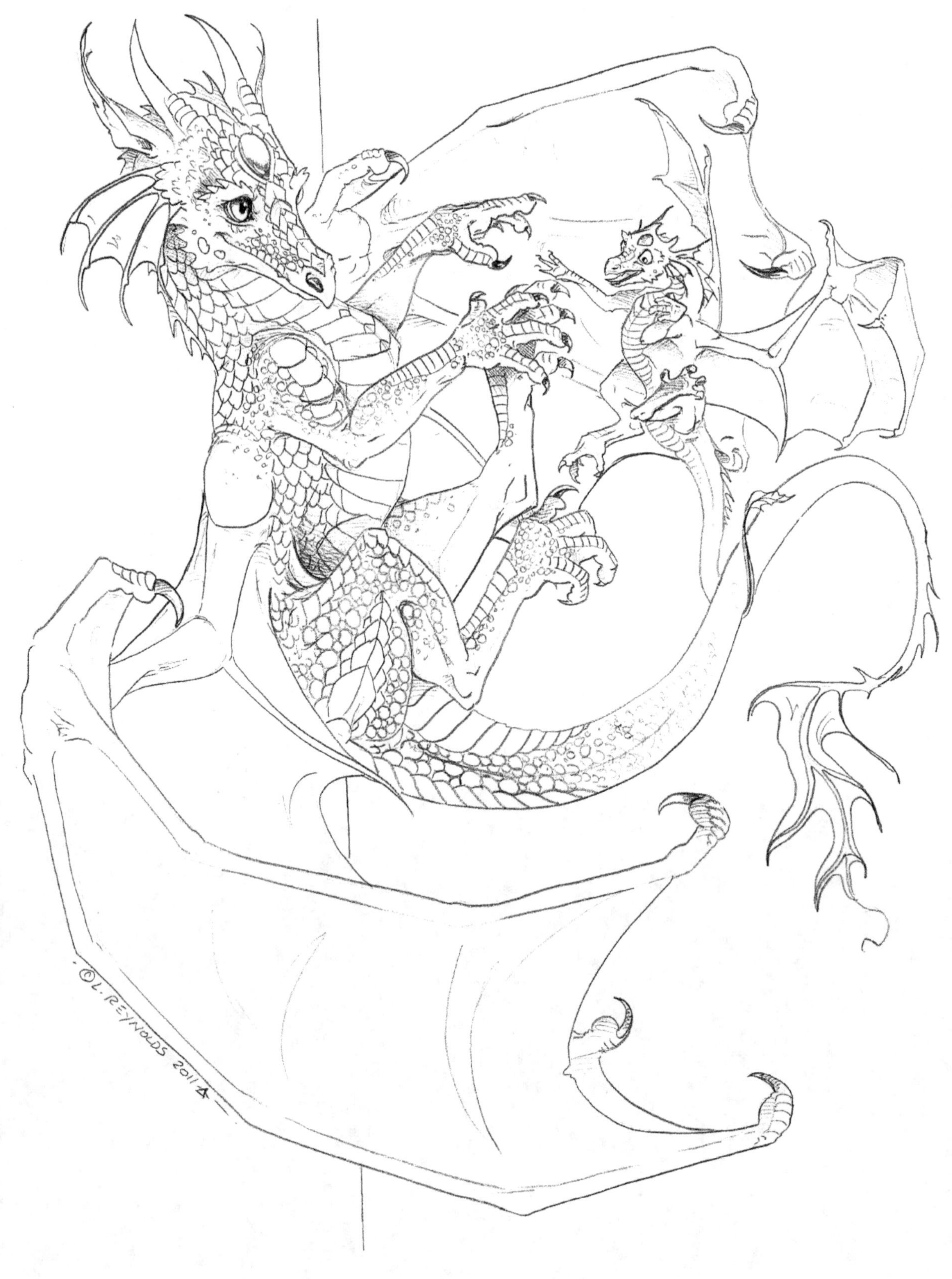
©L. REYNOLDS 2011 4

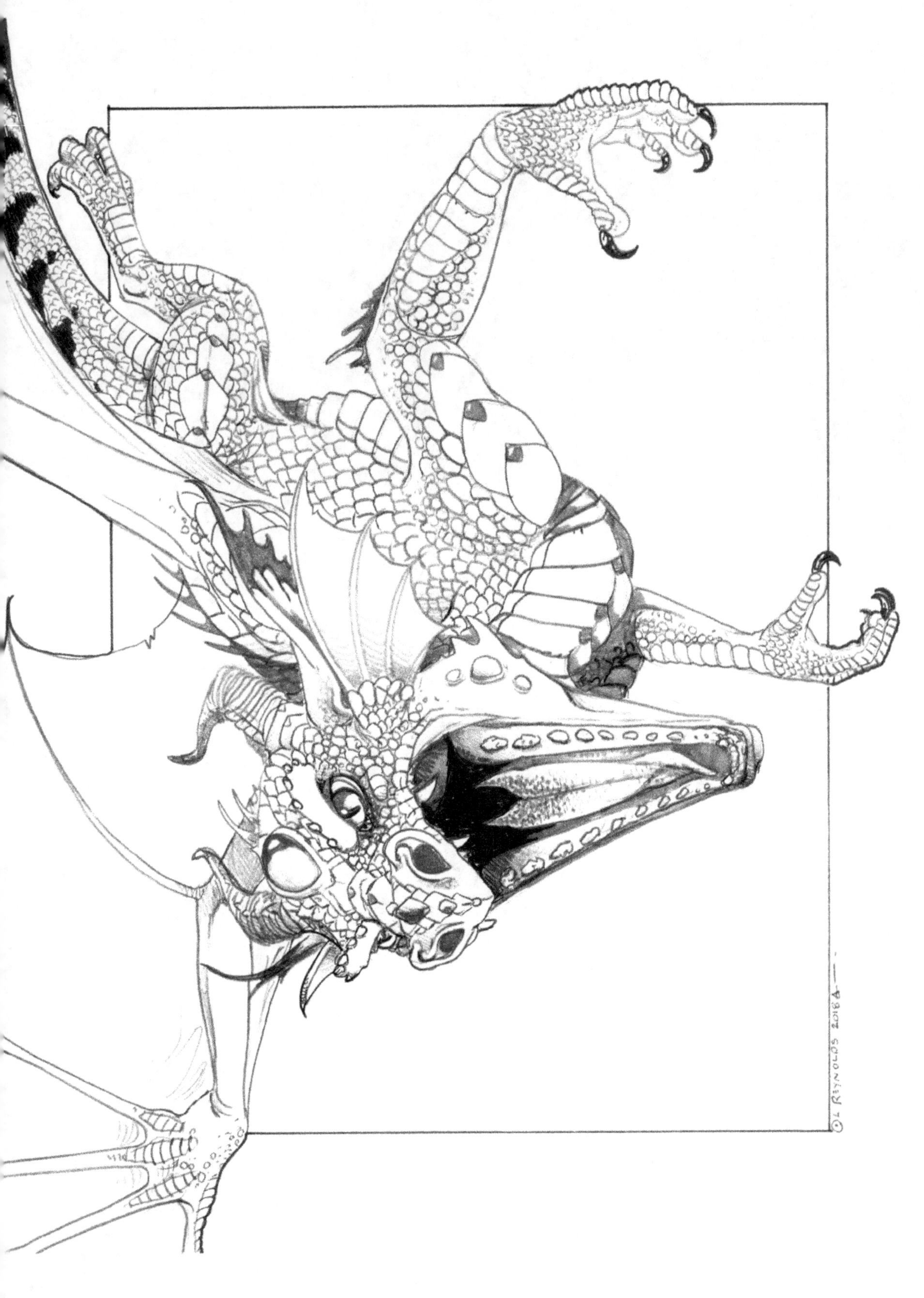

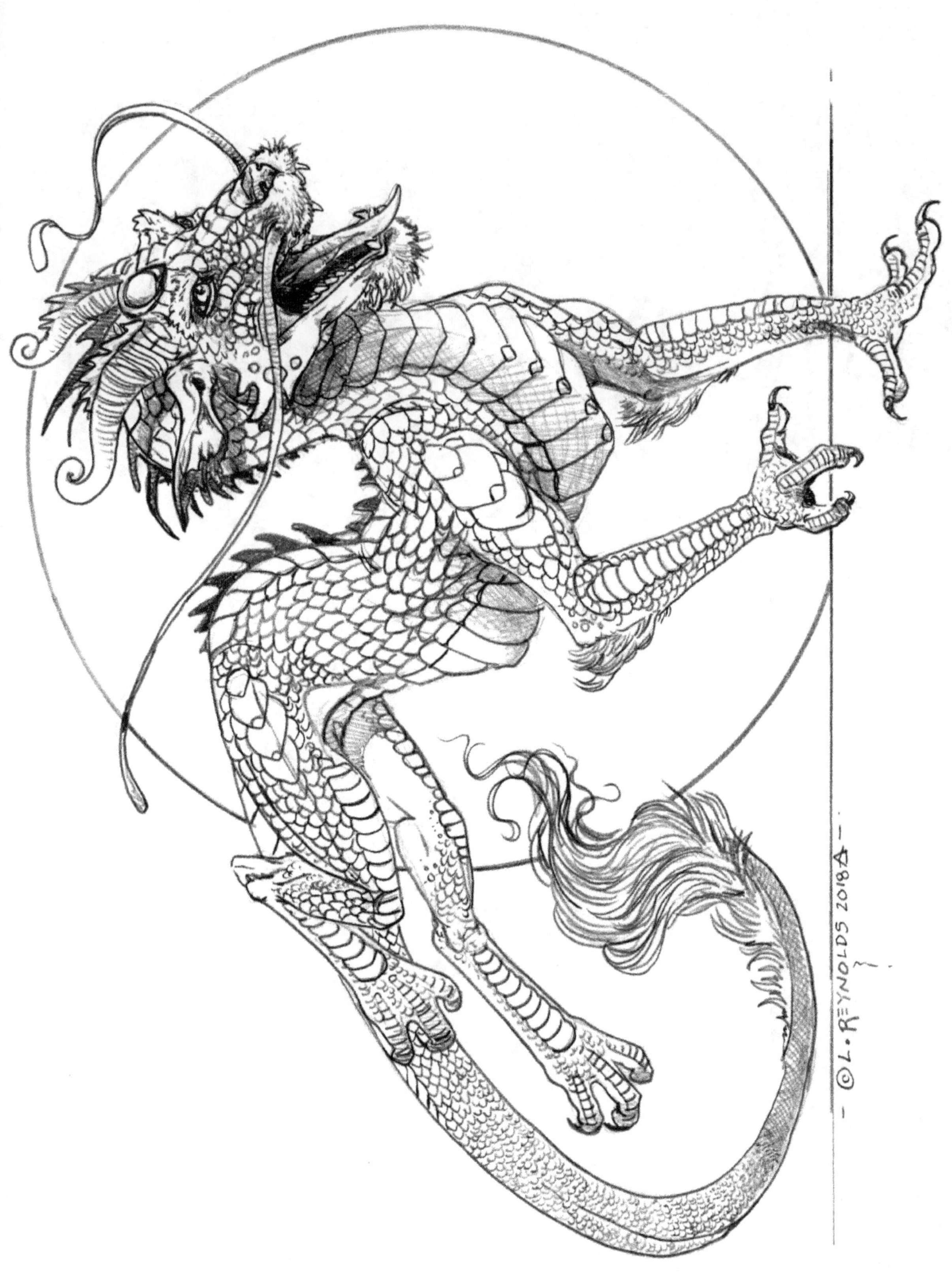

© L. REYNOLDS 2018

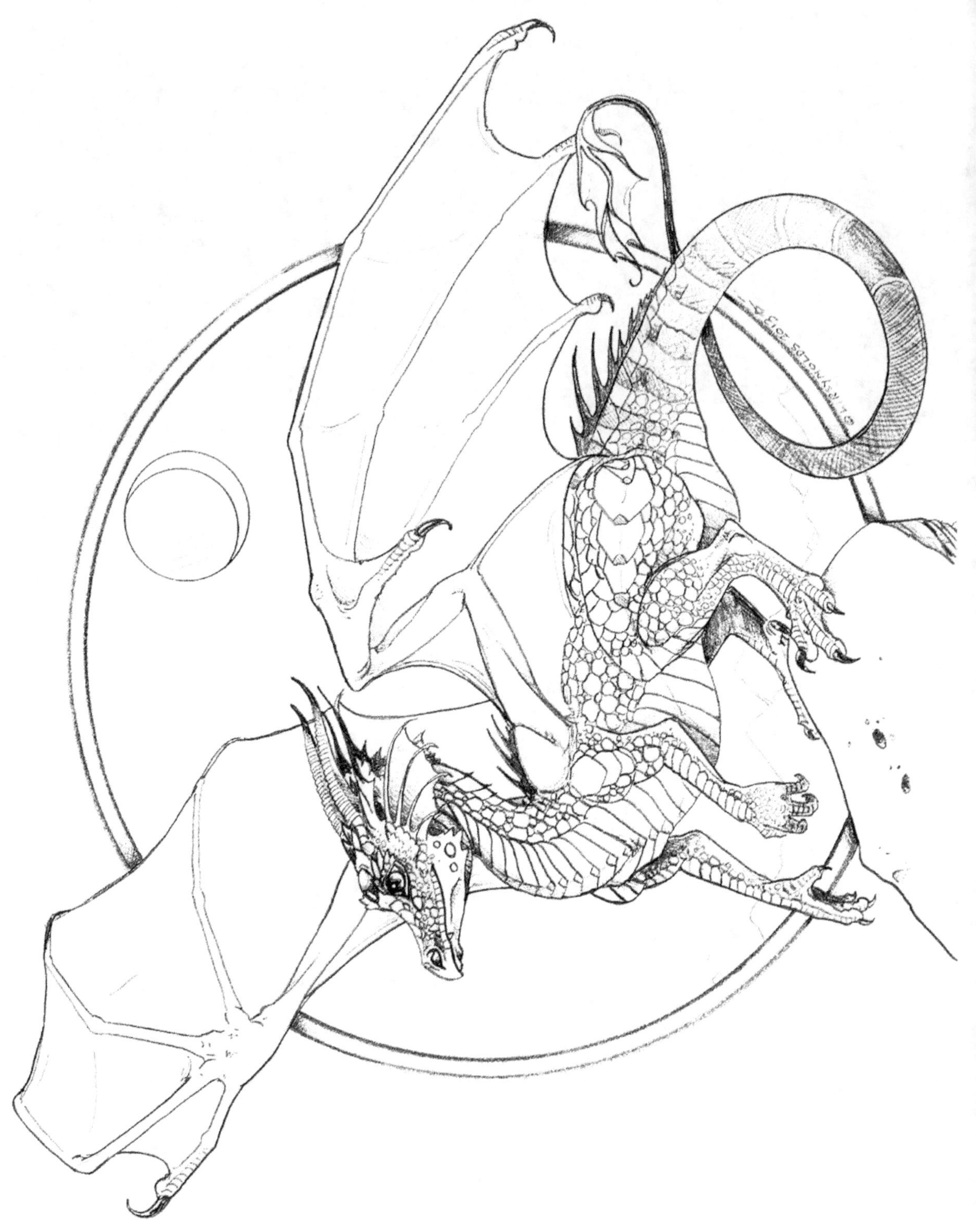

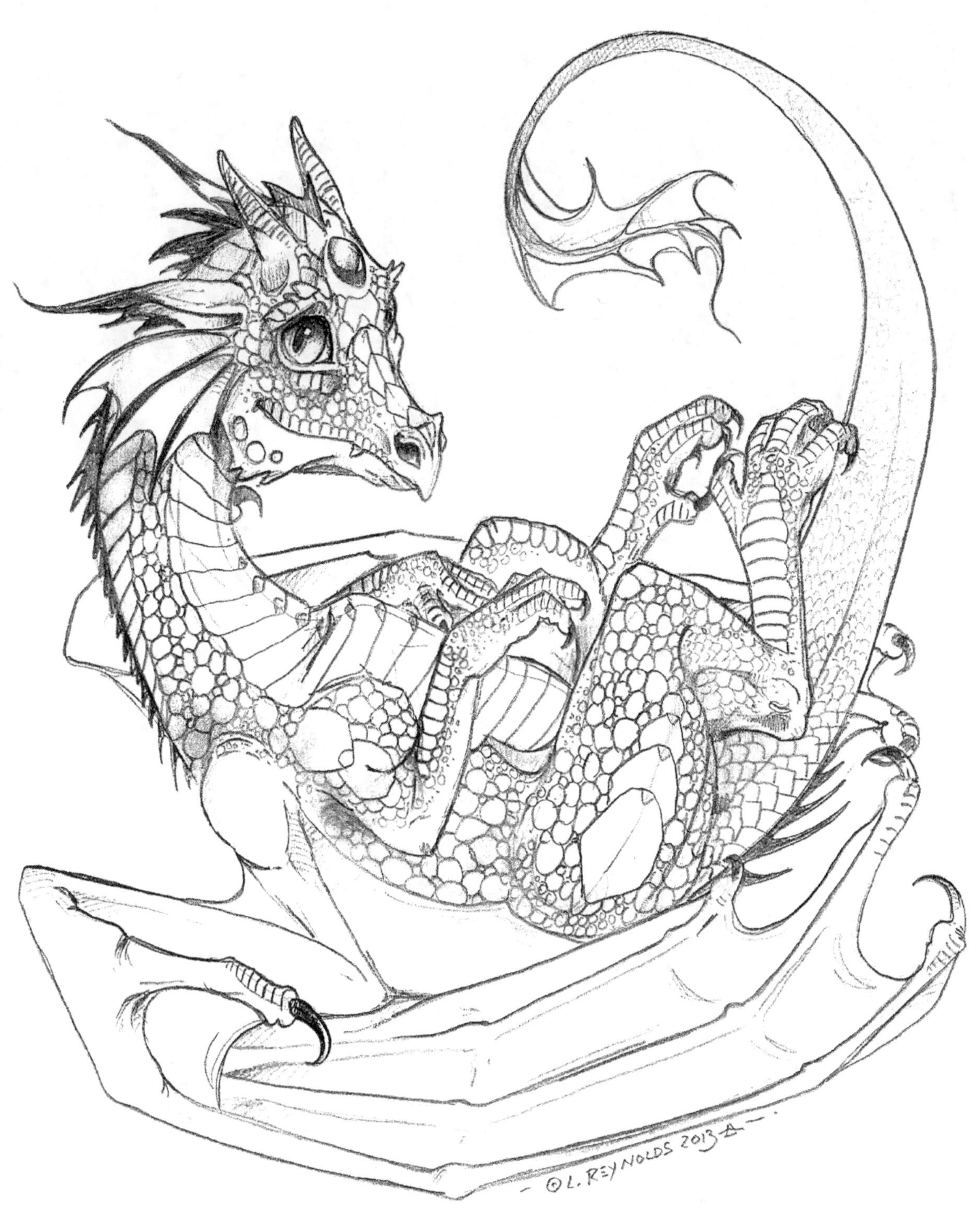
©L. REYNOLDS 2013

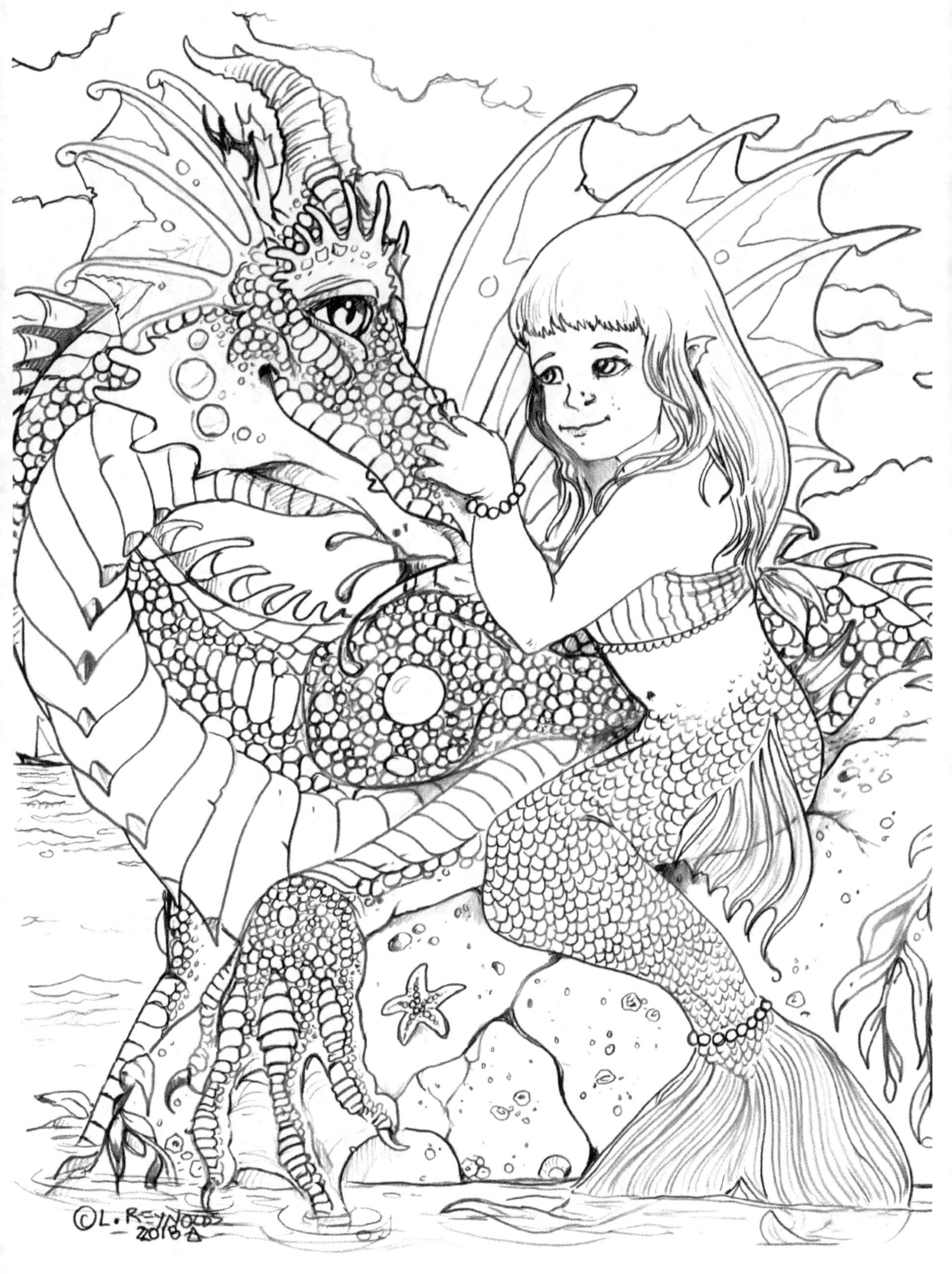
©L. Reynolds
2018

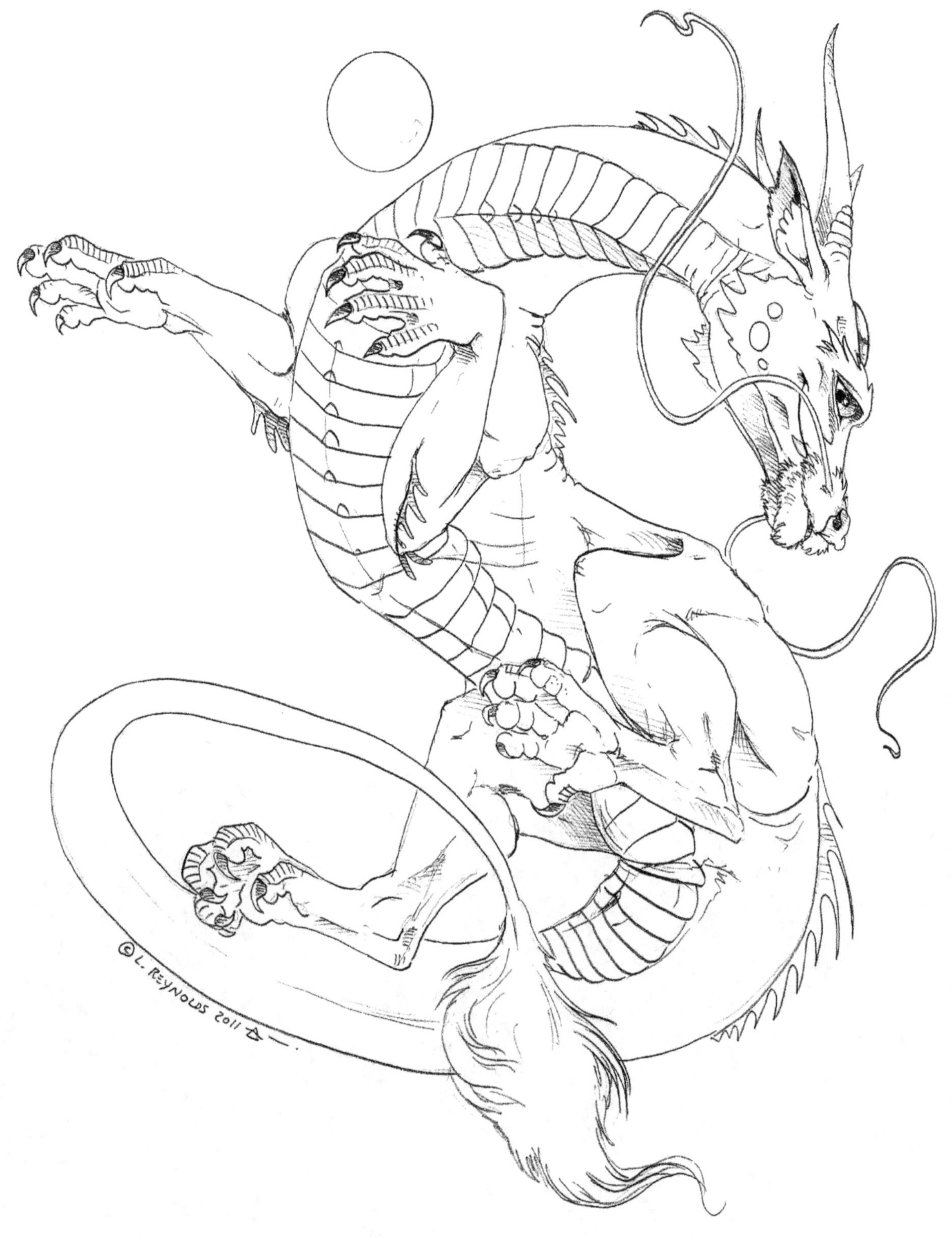
© L. Reynolds 2011

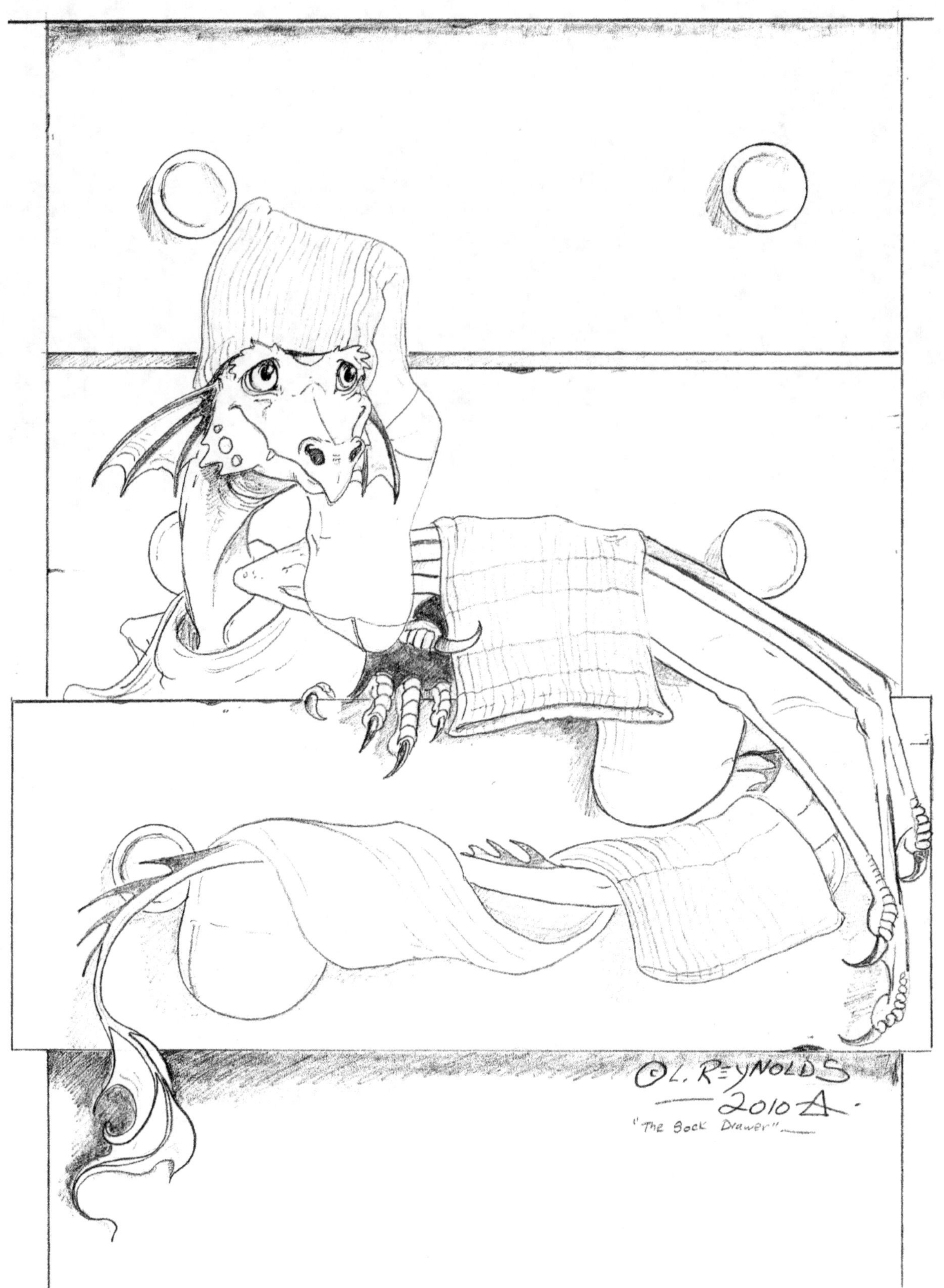
©L. Reynolds
2010
"The Sock Drawer"

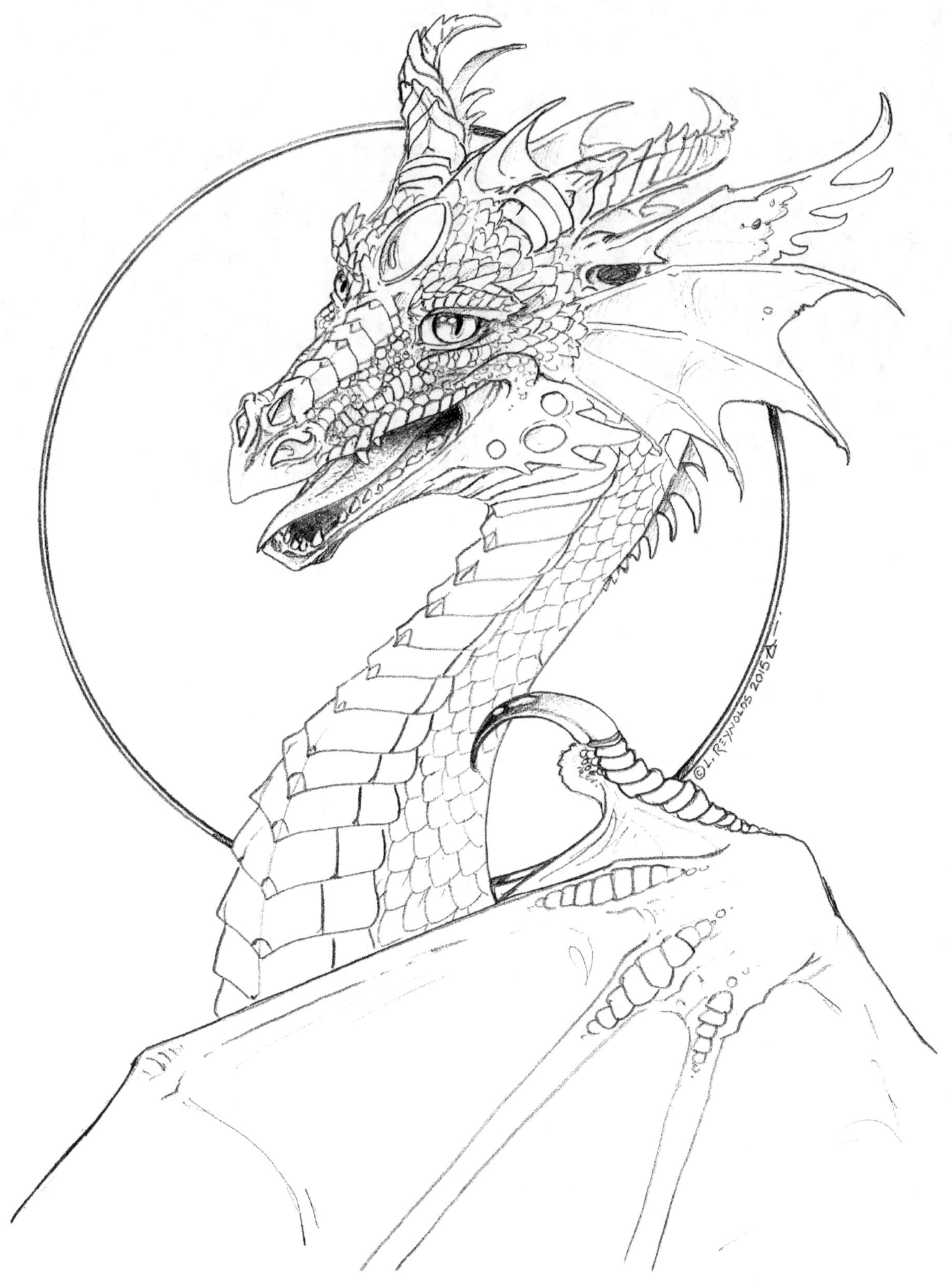

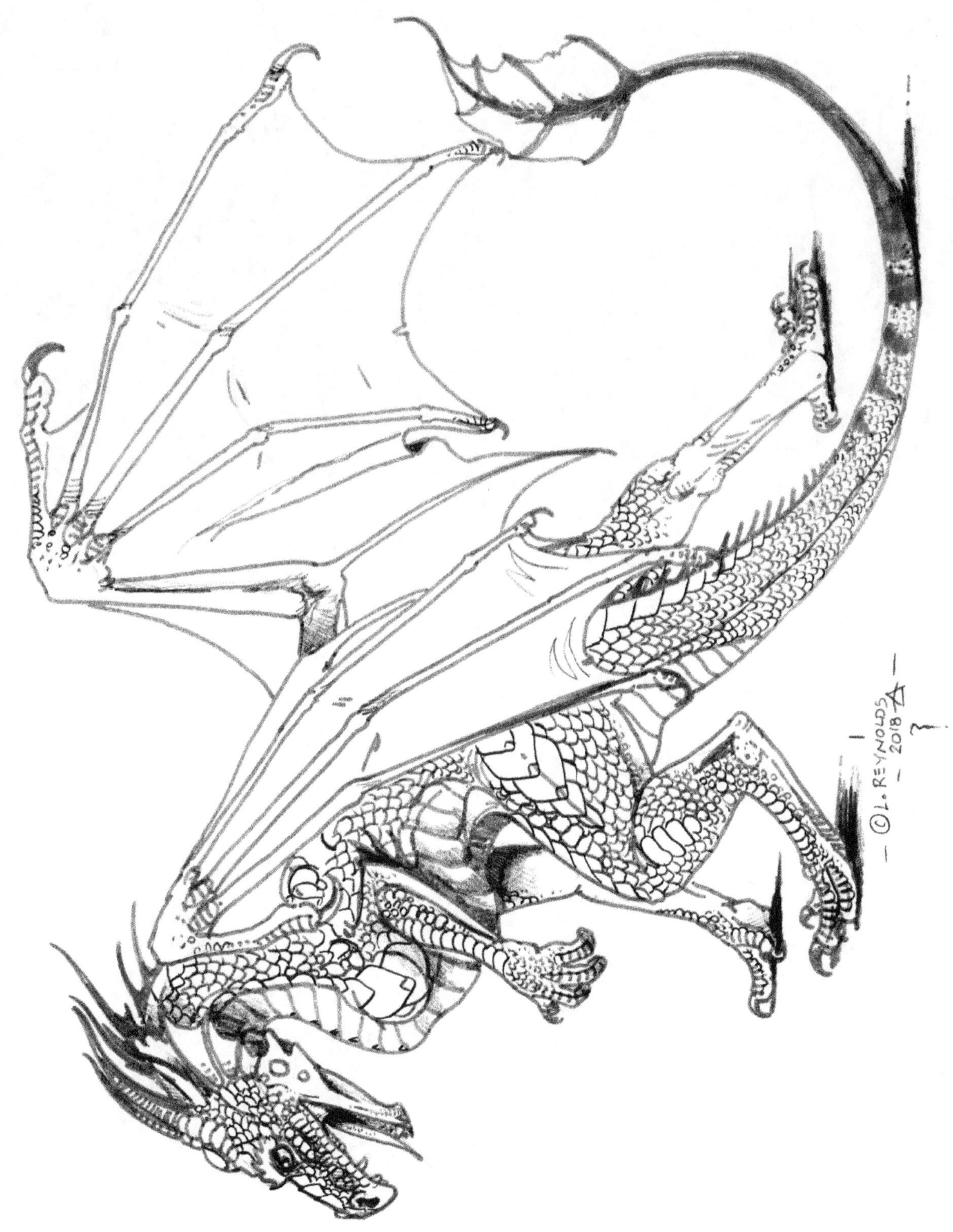

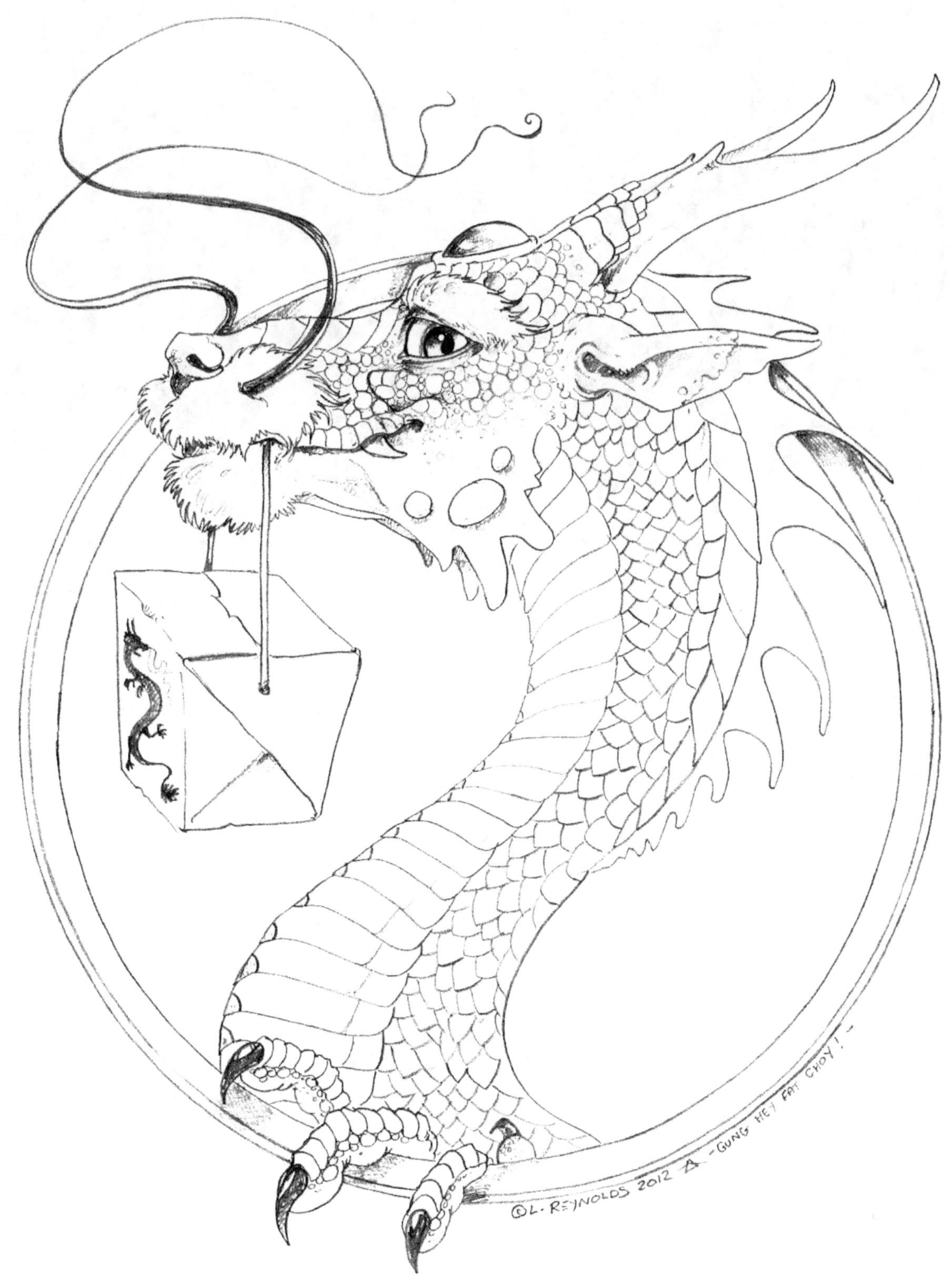

©L. REYNOLDS 2012
- GUNG HEY FAT CHOY! -

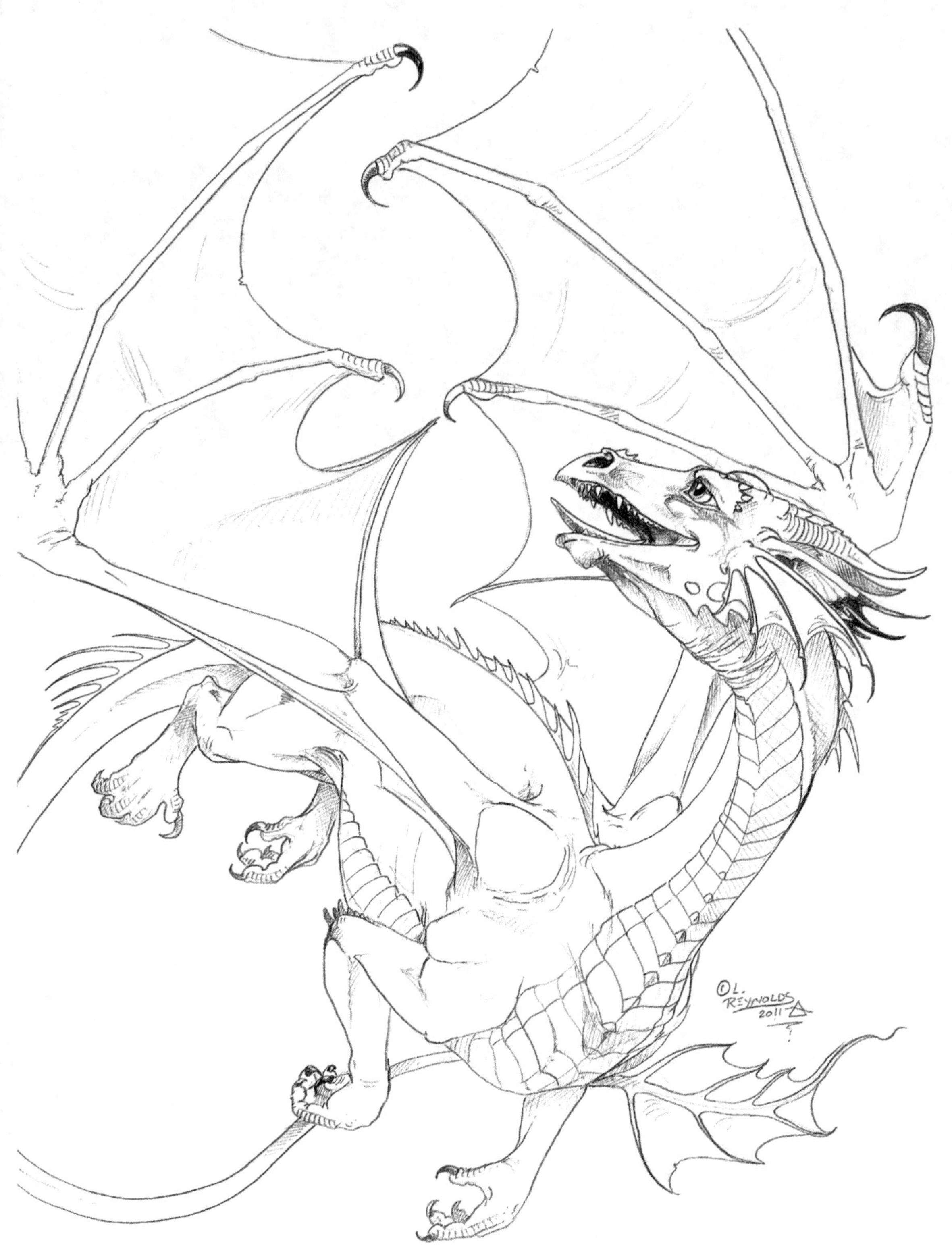

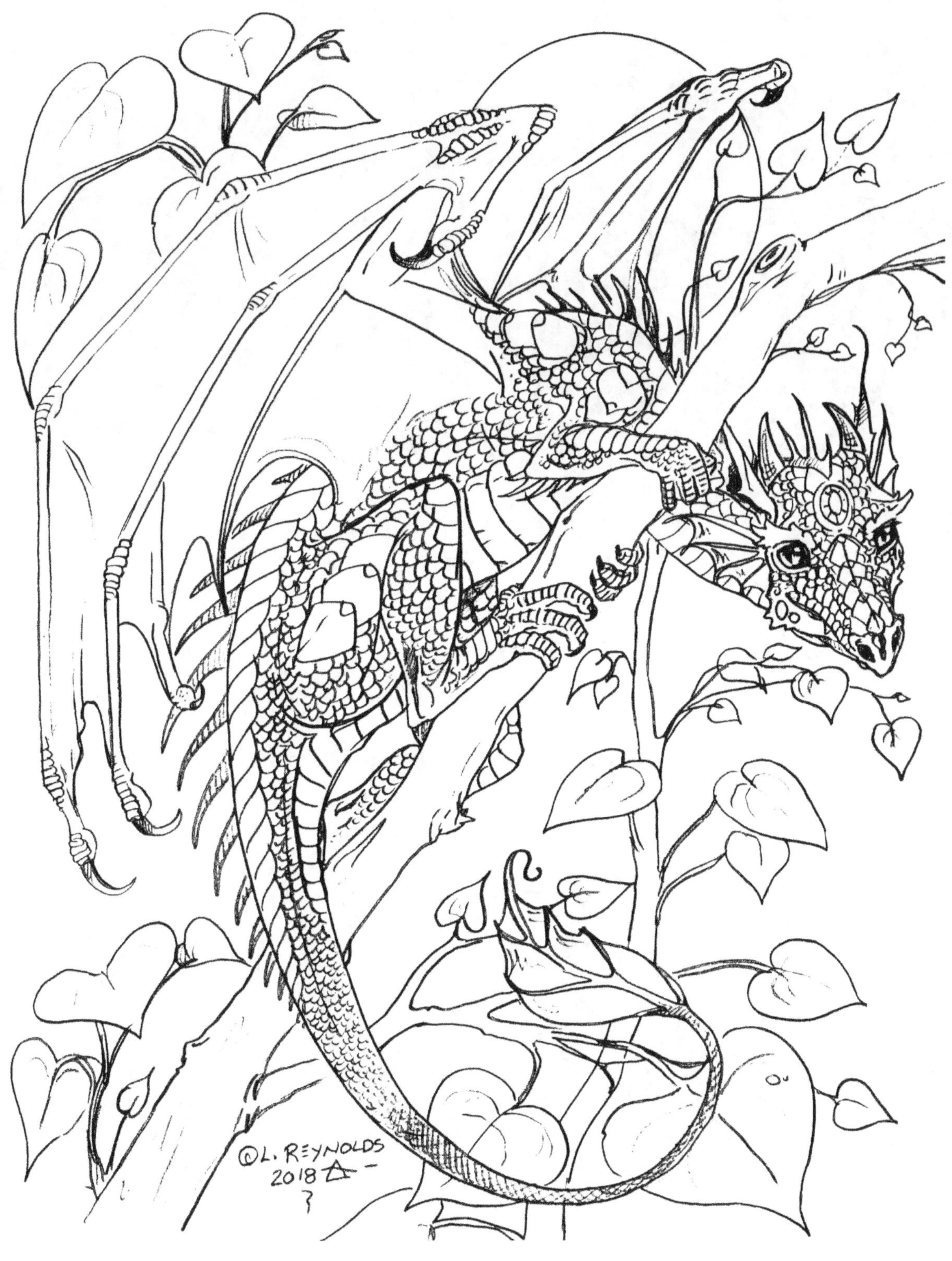
©L. Reynolds
2018

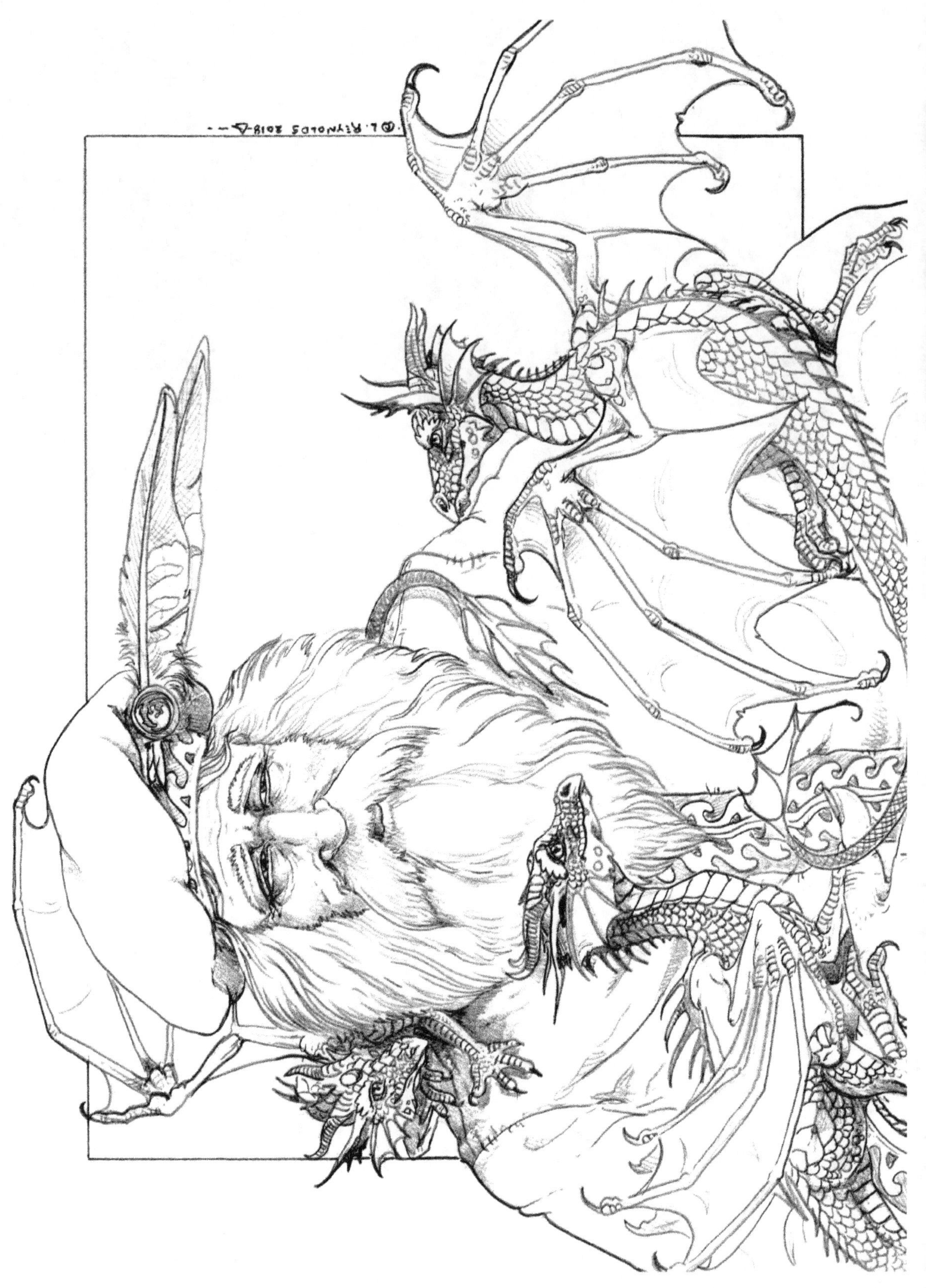

© L. REYNOLDS 2018

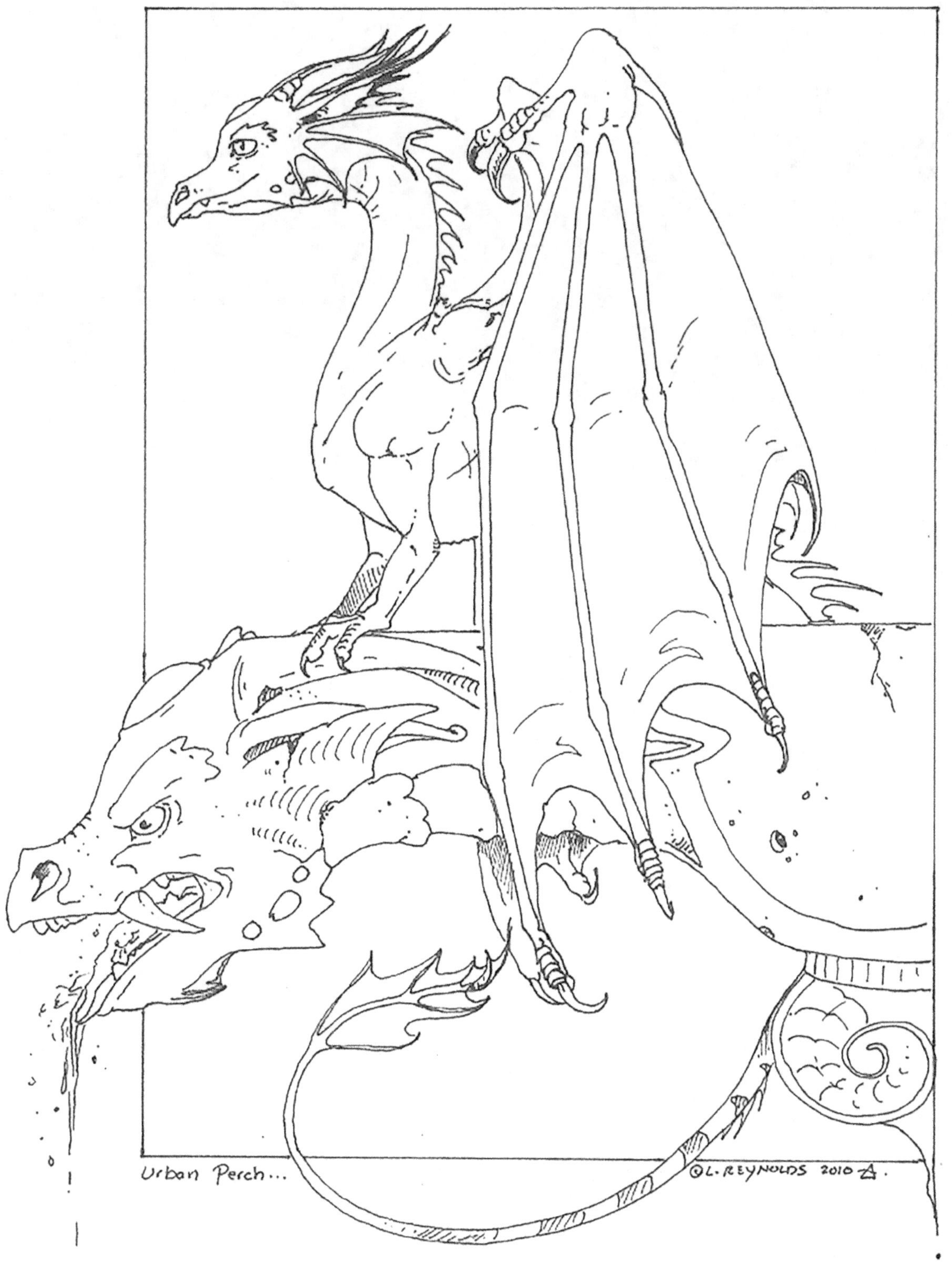

Urban Perch...
©L. REYNOLDS 2010

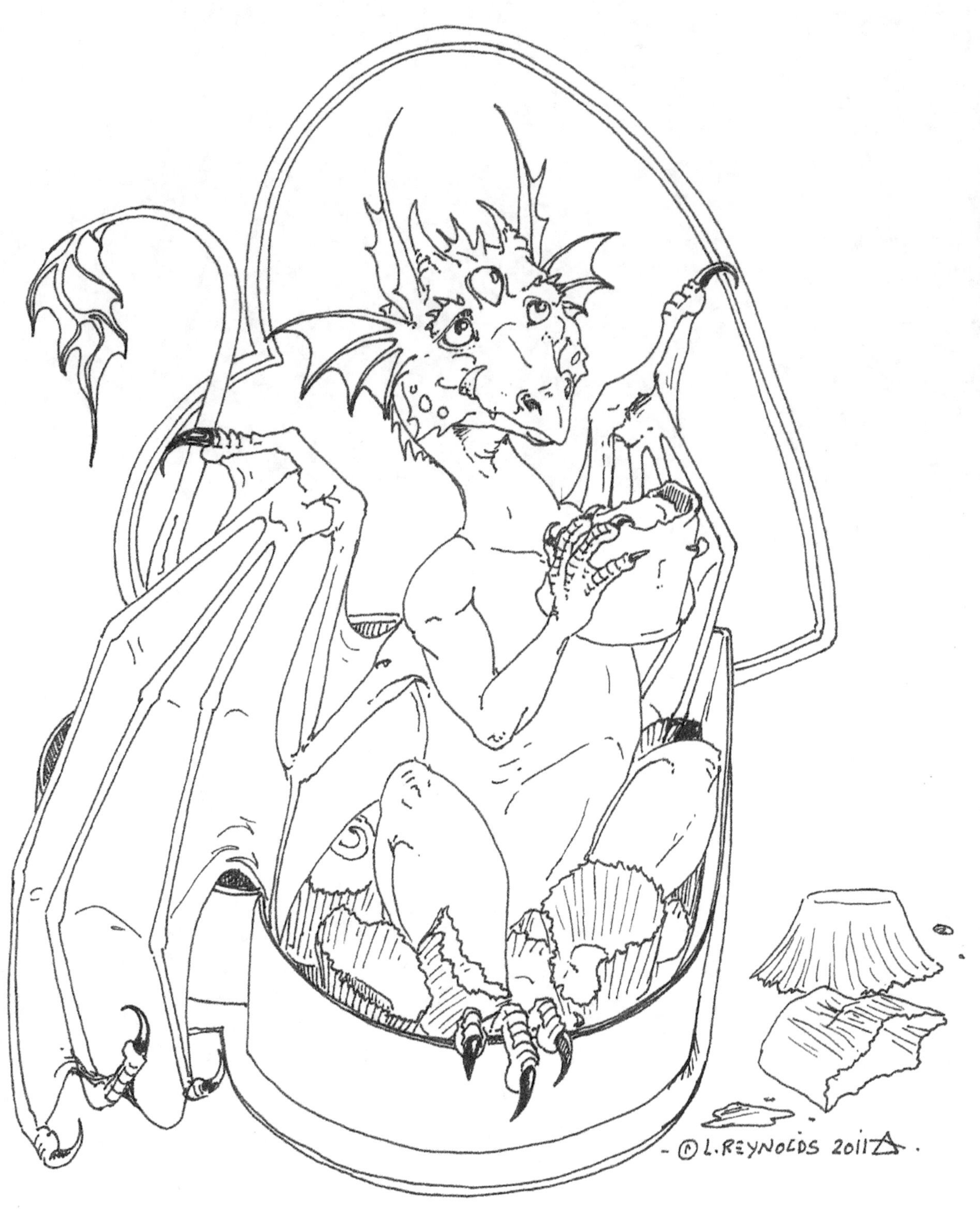

- © L. REYNOLDS 2011 -

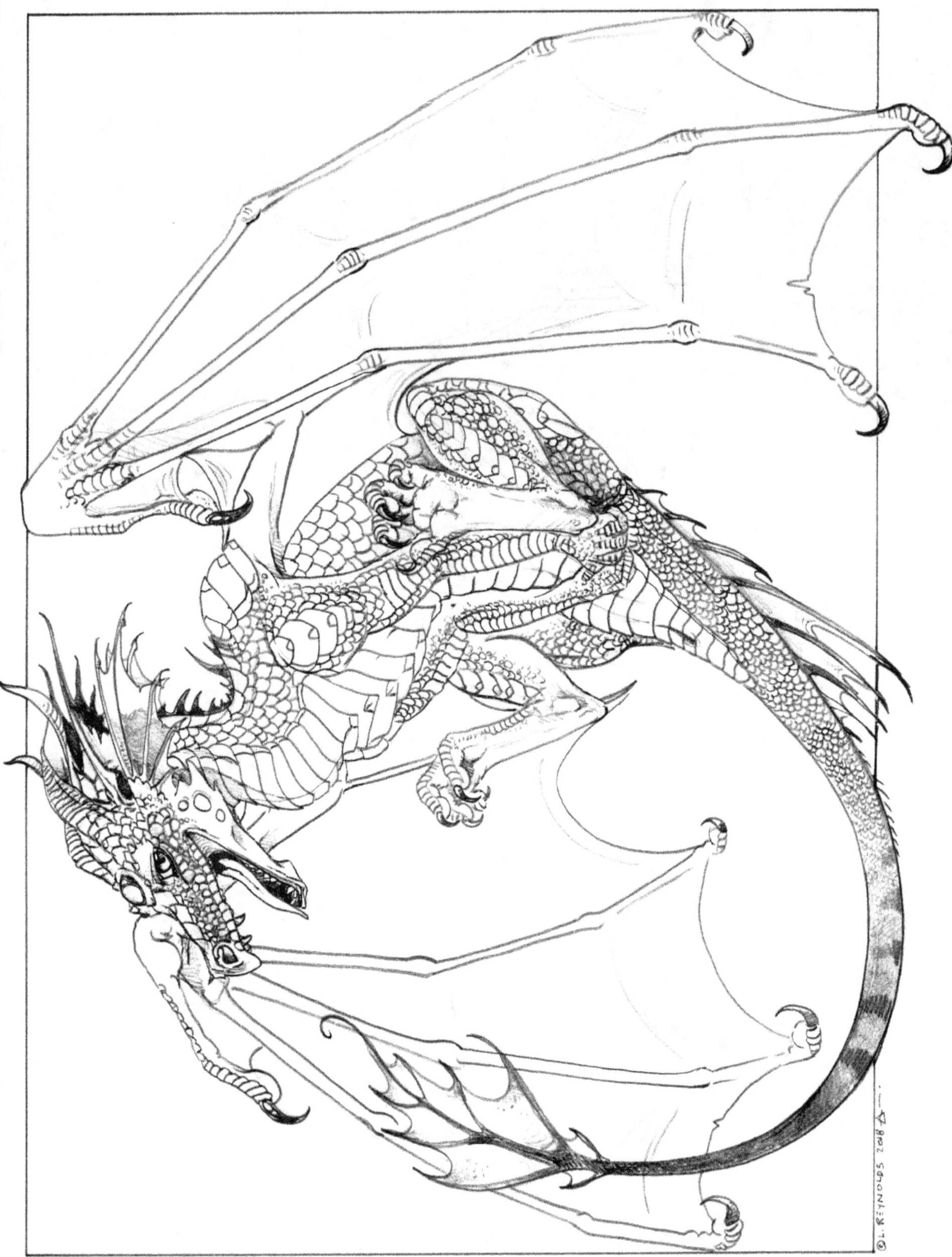

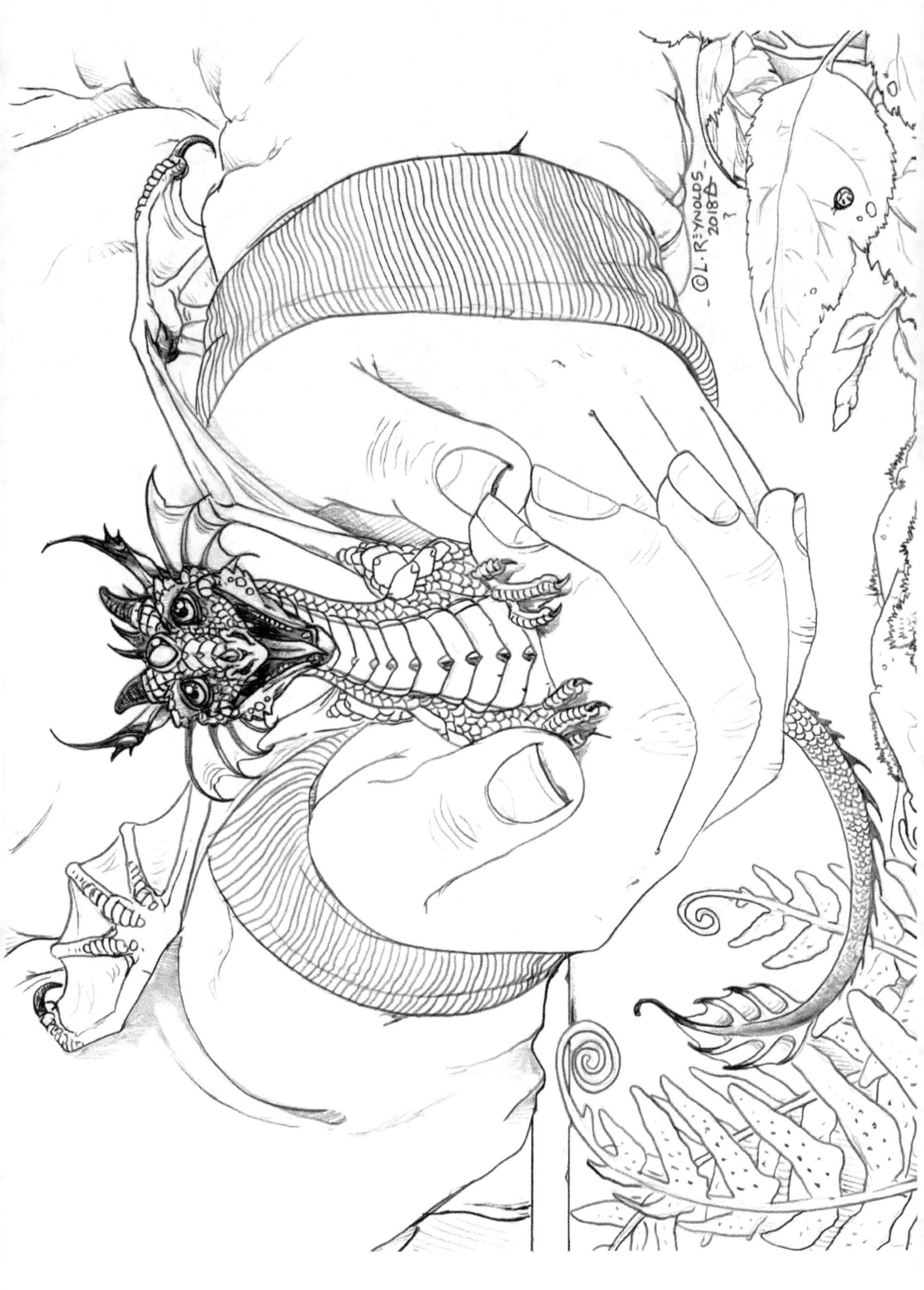

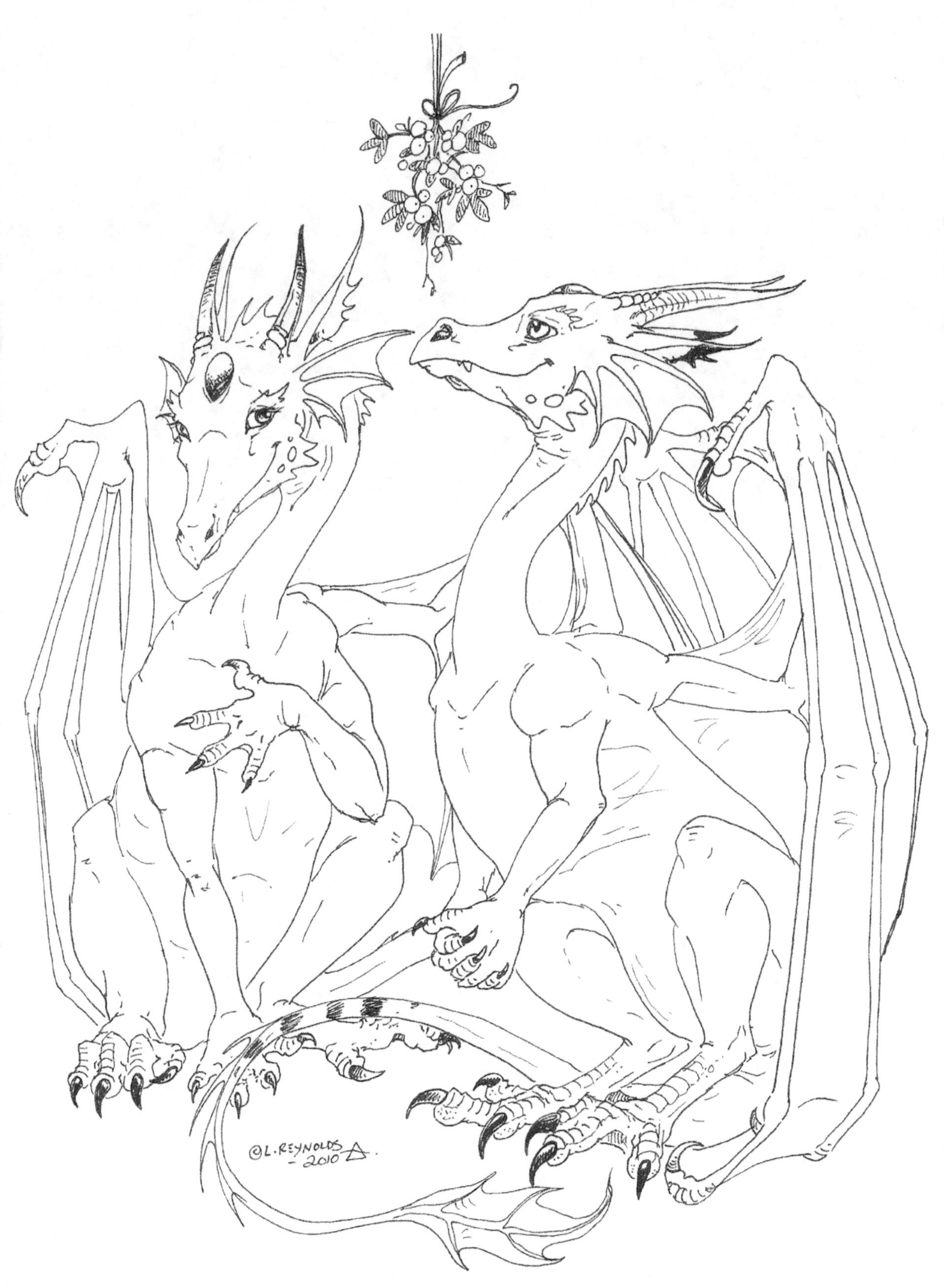
©L.REYNOLDS
- 2010

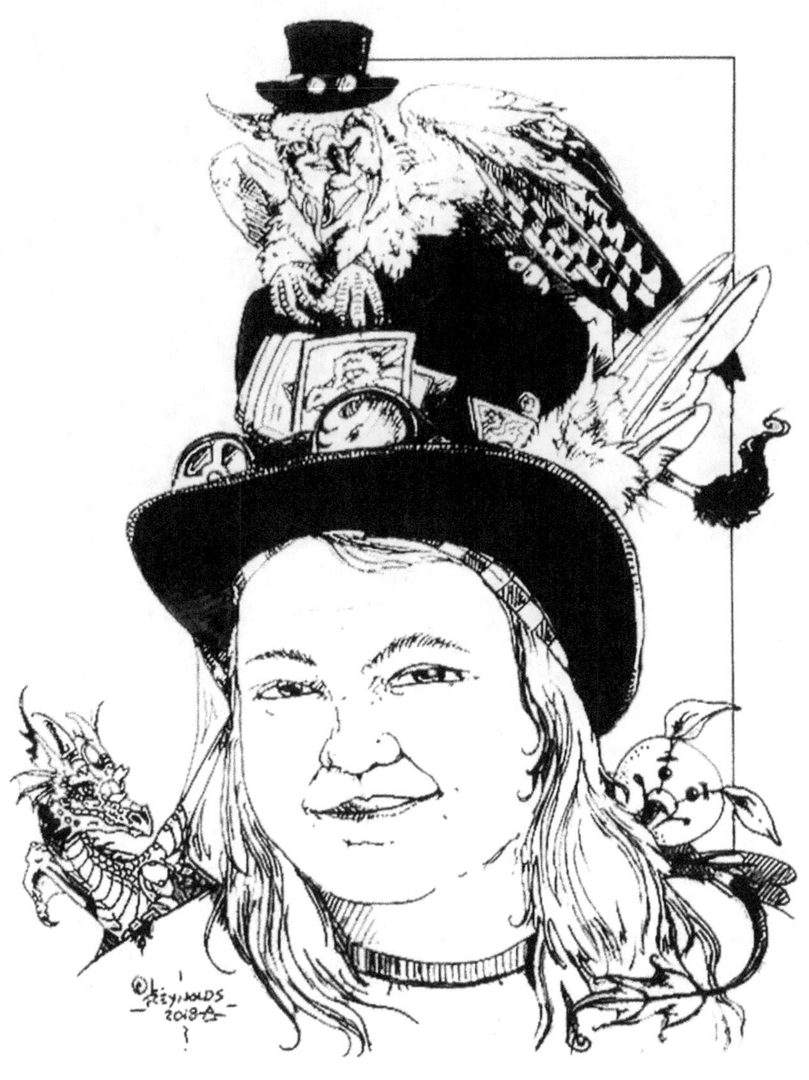

Artist Laura Reynolds, is a studied Cryptozoologist, advocate of hand art, curator of the creative, and self-professed flight freak. One of the longest selling artist at Dragon Con, with a lair load of awards and accolades. Photobombing is her longest creation's (Zephy), stuffed toy, Stuffy.

Look for coloring books with Zephy's and Stuffy's adventures?

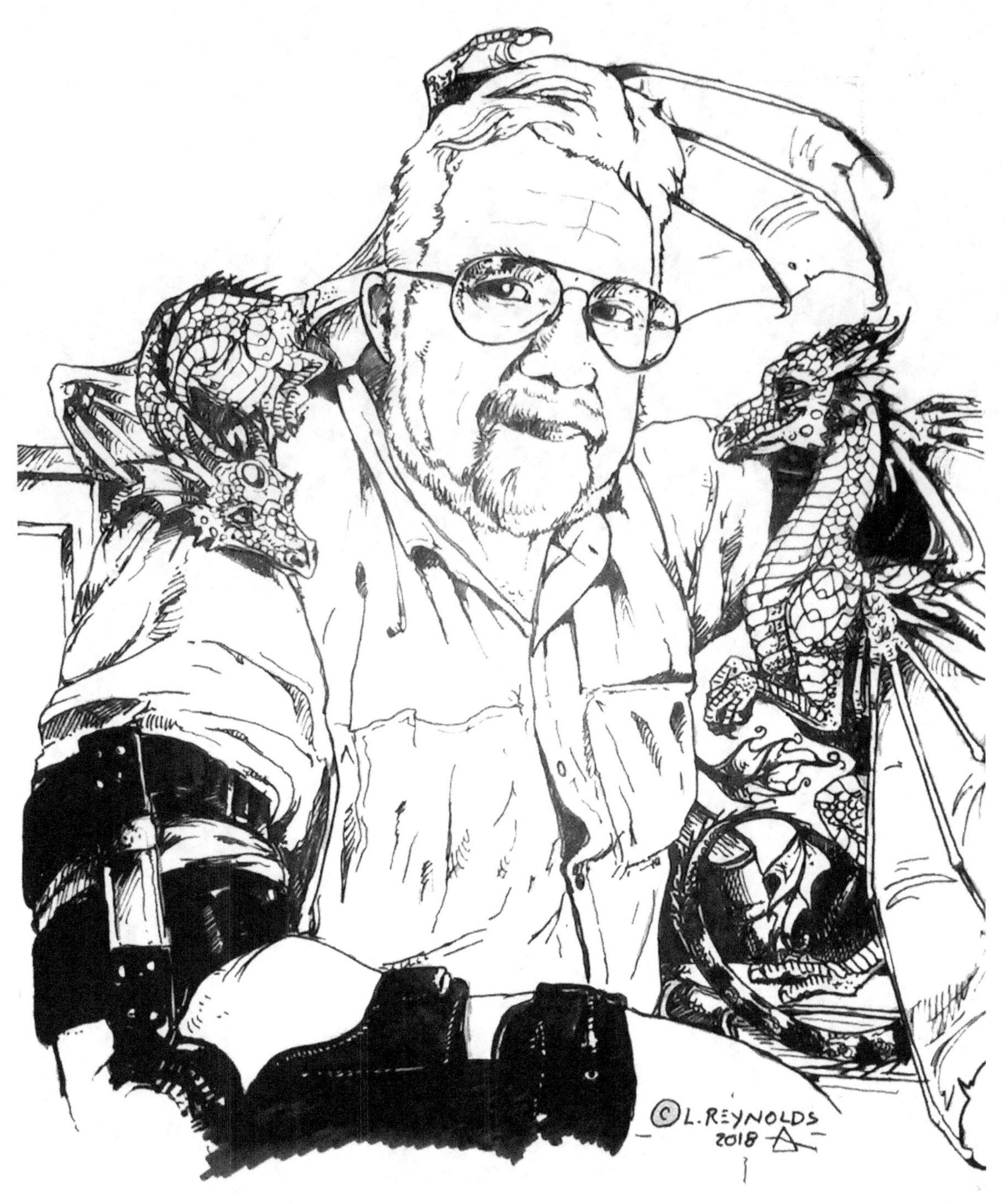

Baer Charlton, publisher, author, and creator of the novel
The Very Littlest Dragon.

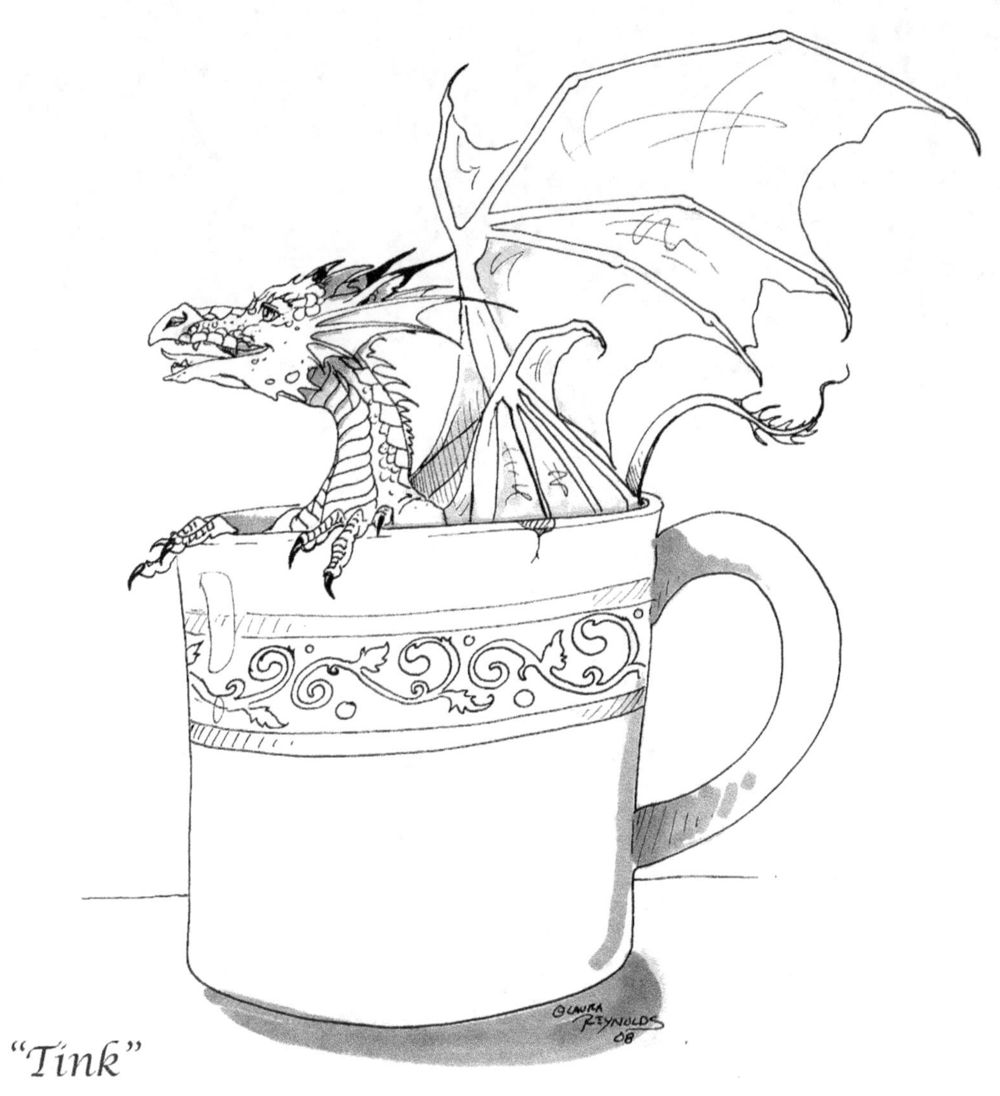

"Tink"

www.ingramcontent.com/pod-product-compliance
Lightning Source LLC
Chambersburg PA
CBHW080401030726
47598CB00010B/2840